100 Prop[illegible]

Commentaries on a selection of Bible prophecies about the Messiah, Israel, other nations, the world, and the future

by George Konig and Ray Konig

3rd Revised Edition

Visit us at www.100prophecies.com

Contents

Introduction

The Bible is unique in many ways. It contains hundreds of prophecies that were recorded during ancient times, by a long list of prophets, involving a variety of subjects.

Some scholars have proposed that there are about 2,000 prophecies in the Bible.

Many of the Bible's prophecies foretold details involving the birth, life, mission, death and resurrection of a Messiah (Jesus Christ). Other Bible prophecies foretold events involving the land and people of Israel, the surrounding nations, and the future of the world.

The Bible's prophets were people who were chosen by God to speak his words. We are told this at different times throughout the Bible, including in this verse:

> In the past God spoke to our forefathers through the prophets at many times and in various ways, but in these last days he has spoken to us by his Son, whom he appointed heir of all things, and through whom he made the universe. (Hebrews 1:1,2, NIV)

This book, *100 Prophecies,* offers our research and commentary on a selection of 100 Bible prophecies.

The first version of this book appeared as an online book during the 1990s. Our material has undergone many changes since then, culminating with this, the third revised edition of *100 Prophecies.*

If you have questions, comments or criticisms about this book, or would like to learn more about related topics, or about the authors, please visit us at 100prophecies.com.

Chapter 1
10 major prophecies

The Bible contains many prophecies regarding the land and people of Israel, the nations surrounding Israel, the future of the world, and the Messiah who would suffer and die for our sins and reign forever as king. This chapter reviews 10 selected prophecies that have had far-reaching fulfillments, many of which are visible and evident to people throughout the world today.

1. A unique religious text

Bible passages: Psalm 48:10; Psalm 22:27; Isaiah 45:22
Written: More than 2,000 years ago

Why is it that the Bible became the world's most widely distributed and most influential book of all time?

What are the odds that a religious text written by a small nation of people would end up shaping the world more than any other book, by any other people, from any other place in the world?

If all things were governed merely by chance, then shouldn't the odds have favored a more ancient society, like that of Egypt, to be the source of the world's most influential book?

Or shouldn't the odds have favored a book from Mesopotamia, a region in western Asia, which is said to be the very cradle of civilization?

Or why not a book from the other side of Asia, which is home to two of the world's oldest and most populous nations - China and India?

Instead, the world's most influential book comes from a tiny nation of people, the people of Israel, who from the time of Moses, until the century in which Jesus lived, were inspired by God to write down the words of the Bible. And these words include assurances and prophecies that information about God would reach the ends of the earth.

We see this in Psalm 48:10, where there is a reference to God being known and praised throughout the world:

> According to thy name, O God, so is thy praise unto the ends of the earth: thy right hand is full of righteousness. (Psalm 48:10, KJV)

We see this also in Psalm 22:27:

> All the ends of the world shall remember and turn unto the LORD: and all the kindreds of the nations shall worship before thee. (Psalm 22:27, KJV)

And we see this in Isaiah 45:22, where the offer of salvation is shown to be for all people, throughout the world:

> Look unto me, and be ye saved, all the ends of the earth: for I am God, and there is none else. (Isaiah 45:22, KJV)

And there are other examples, some of which are discussed elsewhere in this book, that say that God, and his offer of salvation, would become known throughout the world.

Through the spread of Christianity, the Bible became the first religious text to be distributed throughout the world. The Bible, according to commonly used almanac and encyclopedia sources, is the predominant religious text in Europe, Oceania, North America and South America. At least some of these sources of information claim that it also is the predominant religious text in Africa. And, it has an influential presence in Asia, especially in Armenia, East Timor, the nation of Georgia, Hong Kong, the Philippines, Russia, South Korea, and Israel, which is the birthplace of Jesus.

2. The Bible is uniquely associated with prophecy

Bible passage: Isaiah 48:5,6
Written: About 2,700 years ago

Of all the religious texts that have ever been written, the Bible is unique to the extent to which it contains prophecies, and it is unique to the extent to which people associate it with prophecy.

During Biblical times, God chose prophets from among the people of Israel and gave them prophecies - promises - about the future. Through prophecy, God showed that he is in control.

In a passage within the Bible's book of Isaiah, where God is speaking through the prophet Isaiah, God asserts his ability to foretell the future:

> I have even from the beginning declared it to thee; before it came to pass I shewed it thee: lest thou shouldest say, Mine idol hath done them, and my

> graven image, and my molten image, hath commanded them. Thou hast heard, see all this; and will not ye declare it? I have shewed thee new things from this time, even hidden things, and thou didst not know them. (Isaiah 48:5,6, KJV)

According to some estimates, there are about 2,000 prophecies within the Bible.

At least one scholar, J. Barton Payne, has proposed a specific number in the counting of Bible prophecies. In Payne's *Encyclopedia of Biblical Prophecy,* there is a given total of 1,817 Biblical prophecies. That book also proposes that about one-fourth of the Bible's verses contain prophetic content.

3. The Bible foretold a nation

Bible passage: Genesis 15:18
Written: As early as 1400 BC, about 3,400 years ago

The Bible's book of Genesis contains prophecies about what has become the most famous promise of land that the ancient world has to offer.

Shortly after God promises Abraham that he would become patriarch to an uncountable number of descendants (Genesis 15:5), he also promises Abraham that his descendants would inherit the land on which Abraham was standing:

> In the same day the LORD made a covenant with Abram, saying, Unto thy seed have I given this land, from the river of Egypt unto the great river, the river Euphrates: (Genesis 15:18, KJV)

The promise is later passed on through Abraham's son, Isaac, and then through Abraham's grandson, Jacob (Genesis 35:12). Jacob, who later became known as Israel, was the father of 12 sons who became the fathers of the 12 Tribes of Israel.

This prophecy found fulfillment during ancient times. As told in the Bible's book of Joshua, the Israelites conquered portions of the land of Canaan, which became known as Israel, about 3,400 years ago. Centuries later, King David extended the boundaries of Israel.

4. The Bible foretold a nation's history

Bible passages: Several, including Deuteronomy 28
Written: Deuteronomy is attributed to Moses who lived about 3,400 years ago

Many prophecies in the Bible addressed the land and people of Israel. These prophecies are scattered throughout the Bible, in both the Old Testament and New Testament. As a group, these prophecies foretold a cycle of destruction and restoration, involving a variety of events such as:

1. The destruction of Jerusalem and the Temple. (Micah 3:11,12; Daniel 9:26; Luke 21:5,6).

2. The exile of the people of Israel. (Deuteronomy 4:25-27; Deuteronomy 28:36,37; Hosea 9:17).

3. The scattering of the exiles to places throughout the world. (Luke 21:24; Leviticus 26:33; Deuteronomy 28:64).

4. The desolation of the land of Israel. (Leviticus 26:27-33; Deuteronomy 29:23).

5. The persecution of the exiles of Israel. (Deuteronomy

28:37; Deuteronomy 28:65-67).

6. The preservation of the people of Israel. (Jeremiah 30:11).

7. The re-gathering of the people of Israel. (Jeremiah 32:37-41; Isaiah 43:5,6).

8. The restoration of Israel. (Deuteronomy 30:3-5; Ezekiel 36:8-12).

Israel experienced a cycle of destruction and restoration during ancient times, after the Israelites took control of the land about 3,400 years ago.

Internal strife led to the nation splitting up into two kingdoms about 2,900 years ago. The southern kingdom became known as Judah. The northern kingdom retained the name of Israel.

Both kingdoms later fell to invading armies. The Assyrians conquered the northern kingdom about 2,700 years ago, and the Babylonians conquered Judah about 2,600 years ago.

In both instances, many people were forced out of their homeland and into exile. But after the fall of the Neo-Babylonian empire, some exiles began returning to the land of Israel, rebuilding its fallen cities and restoring its land.

By the time of Jesus about 2,000 years ago, Jerusalem was a vibrant city and the Temple had been restored in grand fashion.

Some of the prophecies mentioned above are discussed in greater detail elsewhere in this book.

5. The Bible foretold the fate of other nations

Bible passage: Zephaniah 2:4-10
Written: About 2,600 years ago

There are many prophecies in the Bible that foretold the demise of various nations that were located near the land of Israel during ancient times.

One example can be found in Zephaniah 2:4-10. There, the prophet Zephaniah proclaimed that Moab, Ammon, and Philistia would be destroyed.

In verse 9, we are told that Moab and Ammon, which were east of the Jordan River, would be utterly destroyed, like the more ancient cities of Sodom and Gomorrah.

In verses 4-6, we are told that the people of Philistia would be wiped out. Philistia, which included the cities of Gaza and Ashkelon, bordered Israel and was on the coast of the Mediterranean Sea.

Since the time of Zephaniah, who lived about 2,600 years ago, these nations have lost their sovereignty, culture, and language, as well as their identity as distinct groups of people.

- - -

Here is Zephaniah 2:4-10 (KJV):

4For Gaza shall be forsaken, and Ashkelon a desolation: they shall drive out Ashdod at the noon day, and Ekron shall be rooted up.

5Woe unto the inhabitants of the sea coast, the nation of the Cherethites! the word of the LORD is against you; O Canaan, the land of the Philistines, I will even destroy thee, that there shall be no inhabitant.

6And the sea coast shall be dwellings and cottages for shepherds, and folds for flocks.

7And the coast shall be for the remnant of the house of Judah; they shall feed thereupon: in the houses of Ashkelon shall they lie down in the evening: for the LORD their God shall visit them, and turn away their captivity.

8I have heard the reproach of Moab, and the revilings of the children of Ammon, whereby they have reproached my people, and magnified themselves against their border.

9Therefore as I live, saith the LORD of hosts, the God of Israel, Surely Moab shall be as Sodom, and the children of Ammon as Gomorrah, even the breeding of nettles, and saltpits, and a perpetual desolation: the residue of my people shall spoil them, and the remnant of my people shall possess them.

10This shall they have for their pride, because they have reproached and magnified themselves against the people of the LORD of hosts.

6. The Bible foretold of a 'father of many nations'

Bible passage: Genesis 17:5
Written: As early as 1400 BC, about 3,400 years ago

In the Bible's book of Genesis, we are given a prophecy

involving a man who has become revered as a father of many nations.

His name was Abram, which was later changed to Abraham, and many details of his life are recorded in the Bible's book of Genesis. In chapter 12, we are told that God had spoken to Abram, telling him to leave his people and his country:

> Now the LORD had said unto Abram, Get thee out of thy country, and from thy kindred, and from thy father's house, unto a land that I will shew thee: And I will make of thee a great nation, and I will bless thee, and make thy name great; and thou shalt be a blessing: (Genesis 12:1,2, KJV)

Abram did as he was told and traveled from the land of the Chaldeans to the land of Canaan, which would later become known as Israel. God gave him a promise that he would become the "father of many," indicating that he would be blessed with many descendants:

> Neither shall thy name any more be called Abram, but thy name shall be Abraham; for a father of many nations have I made thee. (Genesis 17:5, KJV)

The name Abraham means "father of many."

Today, Abraham is revered among millions of people as a common ancestor through blood. Many Jews revere him as a forefather through his son Isaac. Many Arabs revere him as a forefather through his son Ishmael.

And many Christians revere him as a spiritual ancestor by sharing his faith:

> Therefore it is of faith, that it might be by grace; to the end the promise might be sure to all the seed; not to that only which is of the law, but to that also which is of the faith of Abraham; who is the father of us all, (Romans 4:16, KJV)

> For ye are all the children of God by faith in Christ Jesus. For as many of you as have been baptized into Christ have put on Christ. There is neither Jew nor Greek, there is neither bond nor free, there is neither male nor female: for ye are all one in Christ Jesus. And if ye be Christ's, then are ye Abraham's seed, and heirs according to the promise. (Galatians 3:26-29, KJV)

One of the noteworthy features of the prophecy found in Genesis 17:5 is the extent of its fulfillment: Abraham, more so than any other person in history, is widely revered as a common ancestor by many different groups of people in many nations throughout the world.

History has provided other examples of people being widely regarded as common ancestors, although not to the same extent as Abraham. Two notable examples include Confucius, a Chinese philosopher who lived about 2,500 years ago, and Genghis Khan, the founder of the Mongol Empire, who lived about 800 years ago.

One estimate claims that nearly 3 million people are descendants of Confucius:

> There are an estimated 2.5 million descendants on the Chinese mainland and 100,000 in the Republic of Korea, with the rest in the United States, Malaysia and Singapore.
> - "DNA test to clarify Confucius confusion," *China Daily, via http://english.peopledaily.com.cn,* June 20, 2006.

As for Khan, he might have more than 16 million descendants:

> An international group of geneticists studying Y-chromosome data have found that nearly 8 percent of the men living in the region of the former Mongol empire carry y-chromosomes that are nearly identical. That translates to 0.5 percent of the male population in the world, or roughly 16 million descendants living today.
> - "Genghis Khan," *National Geographic News,* by Hillary Mayell, Feb. 14, 2003.

As impressive as these examples are, the descendants of Confucius and Khan are far more limited in number, geographic distribution, and in racial diversity, than are the descendants of Abraham, who number well into the hundreds of millions of people all over the world by faith and by blood.

7. The Bible foretold of a Messiah

Bible passage: Isaiah 42:1-9
Written: About 2,700 years ago

The Old Testament of the Bible contains many prophecies about a Messiah. One scholar, Alfred Edersheim, concluded that there at least 456 passages in the Old Testament that Jewish Rabbis have interpreted as being about the Messiah:

> Their number amounts to upwards of 456 (75 from the Pentateuch, 243 from the Prophets, and 138 from the Hagiographa), and their Messianic application is supported by more than 558 references to the most ancient Rabbinic writings.
> - Edersheim, *The Life and Times of Jesus the Messiah.*

The word *Pentateuch* refers to the first five books of the Old Testament. The words *Prophets* and *Hagiographa* refer to other portions of the Old Testament. Edersheim was a Jewish convert to Christianity who lived during the 1800s.

One example of a Messianic prophecy can be found in Isaiah 42:1-9. There, the prophet Isaiah, who lived about 700 years before Jesus was born, spoke of a servant of God who would become a light for the Gentiles (non-Jews) and bring justice to the nations.

This prophecy also described the servant as being gentle and meek (verse 2) and yet having a far-reaching impact, on people throughout the world (verses 1, 4 and 6).

From other chapters of Isaiah, and from other prophecies within the Bible, we learn that the Messiah would be born in Bethlehem (Micah 5:2), that he would suffer and die for the sins of others (Isaiah 52:13-53:12), and that he would be eternal (2 Samuel 7:16 and Isaiah 9:6,7).

Jesus is the only person in history who is widely accepted as being the fulfillment of these Bible prophecies.

Christians believe that Jesus, in accordance with other prophecies in the Bible, is to return in the future when he will judge the living and the dead.

- - -

Here is Isaiah 42:1-9 (KJV):

1 Behold my servant, whom I uphold; mine elect, in whom
my soul delighteth; I have put my spirit upon him: he shall
bring forth judgment to the Gentiles.

2He shall not cry, nor lift up, nor cause his voice to be heard in the street.

3A bruised reed shall he not break, and the smoking flax shall he not quench: he shall bring forth judgment unto truth.

4He shall not fail nor be discouraged, till he have set judgment in the earth: and the isles shall wait for his law.

5Thus saith God the LORD, he that created the heavens, and stretched them out; he that spread forth the earth, and that which cometh out of it; he that giveth breath unto the people upon it, and spirit to them that walk therein:

6I the LORD have called thee in righteousness, and will hold thine hand, and will keep thee, and give thee for a covenant of the people, for a light of the Gentiles;

7To open the blind eyes, to bring out the prisoners from the prison, and them that sit in darkness out of the prison house.

8I am the LORD: that is my name: and my glory will I not give to another, neither my praise to graven images.

9Behold, the former things are come to pass, and new things do I declare: before they spring forth I tell you of them.

8. The Messiah would have a worldwide impact

Bible passages: Micah 5:4; Isaiah 49:6; Acts 1:8
Written: The Old Testament books of Micah and Isaiah were written about 2,700 years ago. The New Testament

book of Acts was written during the first century of this era.

There are various prophecies in the Bible that indicate that the Messiah would be known by people far beyond the boundaries of Israel, that he would affect people throughout the world.

In the Old Testament book of Micah, for example, there is a prophecy about the Messiah that says:

> And he shall stand and feed in the strength of the LORD, in the majesty of the name of the LORD his God; and they shall abide: for now shall he be great unto the ends of the earth. (Micah 5:4, KJV)

Another example can be found in the book of Isaiah, where God reveals the impact that the Messiah would have:

> And he said, It is a light thing that thou shouldest be my servant to raise up the tribes of Jacob, and to restore the preserved of Israel: I will also give thee for a light to the Gentiles, that thou mayest be my salvation unto the end of the earth. (Isaiah 49:6, KJV)

About 700 years after the time of the prophets Micah and Isaiah, Jesus was born in the land of Israel. He began his ministry when he was about 30 years old and he proclaimed that he was the Messiah who had been promised by the prophets of the Old Testament.

Jesus also revealed that his followers, who were evangelizing to others about Jesus, would be successful in reaching people throughout the world:

> But ye shall receive power, after that the Holy Ghost is come upon you: and ye shall be witnesses unto me both in Jerusalem, and in all Judaea, and in Samaria,

> and unto the uttermost part of the earth. (Acts 1:8, KJV)

Jesus' followers risked their lives to tell others about Jesus and of the salvation that is found in him. Jesus' followers traveled throughout the Roman Empire, where Christianity was not a legally recognized religion, and beyond. They preached to people throughout parts of Africa, Asia and Europe. From there, Christianity eventually spread to the world's other continents and islands.

The extent to which Jesus is internationally known is unprecedented. Christianity has a widespread, historically influential presence on each of the world's inhabitable continents.

9. Jesus proclaimed that he is the Messiah

Bible passage: Matthew 5:17
Written: During the first century AD, about 2,000 years ago

In Matthew 5:17, Jesus proclaimed that he is the fulfillment of Old Testament prophecies:

> Think not that I am come to destroy the law, or the prophets: I am not come to destroy, but to fulfil. (Matthew 5:17, KJV)

He made similar announcements during other times of his ministry about 2,000 years ago, as recorded in the New Testament. One example can be found in John 4:25,26, where Jesus informed a Samaritan woman that he is the Messiah. Another example can be found in Luke 24:44, where Jesus again spoke of being the subject of Old Testament prophecy.

The Old Testament was written over a period of time that lasted as many as a thousand years, from the time of Moses, who lived about 3,400 years ago, until the time of Malachi, who lived about 2,400 years ago. During that time, Moses, Malachi, and many other Bible prophets gave prophecies involving a Messiah.

Although many people throughout history have claimed to be the Messiah, none, other than Jesus, were able to be taken seriously as being the fulfillment of the Old Testament prophecies about a Messiah.

The Old Testament contains as many as a thousand years worth of prophecy about a Messiah, and Jesus is unique to the extent to which he is acknowledged as being the fulfillment of those promises.

Jesus is also unique to the extent to which his followers were willing to tell others about him, even at the risk of death. His followers wrote the 27 books of the New Testament, during the first century of this era, which is the century in which Jesus lived. The New Testament explains the life, mission, teachings, death and resurrection of Jesus, the Messiah.

10. Jesus prophesied about himself, his followers, his homeland, and the future

Bible passages: Several throughout the New Testament
Written: The New Testament was written during the first century of this era, about 2,000 years ago

Aside from being the fulfillment of Old Testament prophecies, Jesus also gave prophecies.

He gave prophecies about himself, including that he would be rejected, executed, and resurrected.

He gave prophecies about his followers, including that they would be persecuted and that they would be successful in preaching the Gospel throughout the world.

He also gave prophecies involving his homeland, including that Jerusalem would be destroyed, that the Temple would be demolished, and that the Jews would be forced into exile and scattered throughout the nations.

And he gave prophecies about the future, including that his words would persevere and that he would return again in the future.

These examples and others are explained in more detail elsewhere in this book.

Chapter 2
10 prophecies fulfilled by Israel

Many Bible prophecies focus on the land and people of Israel. Collectively, the 10 prophecies selected for review in this chapter describe a series of events that include the establishment of Israel as a nation, the destruction of Jerusalem and the Temple, the exile and dispersion of the people, as well as the preservation and restoration of the land and people.

11. God chooses a man, a land, and a plan

Bible passage: Genesis 12:1-7
Written: As early as 1400 BC, about 3,400 years ago

Throughout the Bible we learn how God had chosen and shaped a people and a land as part of a plan involving salvation.

Much of that choosing and shaping began with a man named Abraham. In Genesis 12:1-7, God told Abraham to leave his country and to travel to the land of Canaan. He told Abraham that a great nation would come from him, that his offspring would inherit the land of Canaan, and that people throughout the world would be blessed through him.

The promises found fulfillment later in history. Abraham, who lived about 4,000 years ago, became the forefather of the nation of Israel. His descendants were chosen by God to receive the words of God and to record them in the Bible. And it was from this nation of people that the world's most influential person was born, the Messiah, Jesus Christ.

Here is Genesis 12:1-7 (KJV):

1 Now the LORD had said unto Abram, Get thee out of thy
country, and from thy kindred, and from thy father's house,
unto a land that I will shew thee:

2 And I will make of thee a great nation, and I will bless
thee, and make thy name great; and thou shalt be a
blessing:

3 And I will bless them that bless thee, and curse him that
curseth thee: and in thee shall all families of the earth be
blessed.

4 So Abram departed, as the LORD had spoken unto him;
and Lot went with him: and Abram was seventy and five
years old when he departed out of Haran.

5 And Abram took Sarai his wife, and Lot his brother's son,
and all their substance that they had gathered, and the souls
that they had gotten in Haran; and they went forth to go
into the land of Canaan; and into the land of Canaan they
came.

6 And Abram passed through the land unto the place of
Sichem, unto the plain of Moreh. And the Canaanite was
then in the land.

7 And the LORD appeared unto Abram, and said, Unto thy

seed will I give this land: and there builded he an altar unto the LORD, who appeared unto him.

12. Israel would become a nation

Bible passage: Genesis 28:10-15
Written: As early as 1400 BC, about 3,400 years ago

Some 4,000 years ago a young man hurried across an expanse of land, bringing a great distance between him and the threat of death that awaited him in the town of his home. Weary from his travel, he lowered himself to the ground and rested his head on a rock.

He slept and dreamt of a future far removed from the conflict that had haunted him that day. His name was Jacob and he was fleeing from his brother Esau, who had sworn to kill him. Jacob had reason to fear his brother. Esau was known for his skills as a hunter and for his acumen in the wild.

Jacob, in contrast, was known more for staying close to the tents of the family's settlement, within the land of Canaan.

For a fight to the death, Jacob might seem outclassed. But as the events of this conflict ran their course, the brothers reversed their roles. Whereas Jacob fled into the wilderness, to escape his brother's wrath, Esau stayed close to home, choosing not to pursue him.

Although they were twins, born only moments apart, Esau was born first. And it was the first-born son who was to be specially treated when it came to matters such as inheritance. But Jacob deceived their blind-and-ailing father, who then gave Jacob the blessings that traditionally would have gone to the first-born son.

Esau vowed to kill his brother. Jacob fled.

In time, Jacob would prevail. He would survive the anger of his brother. And the land from which he was fleeing would one day carry his name, and not that of his brother.

The night that Jacob rested his head on a rock and slept in the wilderness was the night that he dreamt a vision known as "Jacob's Ladder." In this vision, he was told, among other things, that his descendants - none of whom had been born yet - would inherit the land on which he slept.

Jacob's name was later changed to Israel, as was the land beneath him.

This was the land that God had promised to the descendants of Jacob's father, Isaac, and Jacob's grandfather, Abraham. And now, God was promising it to their descendants through Jacob/Israel. This is the land that became the homeland of the Israelites, the people who would record the words of the Bible. And this is the land that became the birthplace of the Messiah, a descendant of Jacob.

This is the land from which Christianity would spread throughout the world, to a vast array of people who look back upon Israel as the Holy Land, the land of the Bible, the land of the Messiah.

Jacob/Israel became the father of the 12 Tribes of Israel. His descendants later conquered the land, seizing control of it about 3,400 years ago from the various groups of people who resided there. The conquest is described in the Bible's Old Testament book of Joshua. Some of the other books of the Old Testament speak of the history that followed, the centuries during which the Israelites lived and prospered within the land of Israel, the land where Jacob dreamed.

Here is Genesis 28:10-15 (KJV):

10And Jacob went out from Beersheba, and went toward Haran.

11And he lighted upon a certain place, and tarried there all night, because the sun was set; and he took of the stones of that place, and put them for his pillows, and lay down in that place to sleep.

12And he dreamed, and behold a ladder set up on the earth, and the top of it reached to heaven: and behold the angels of God ascending and descending on it.

13And, behold, the LORD stood above it, and said, I am the LORD God of Abraham thy father, and the God of Isaac: the land whereon thou liest, to thee will I give it, and to thy seed;

14And thy seed shall be as the dust of the earth, and thou shalt spread abroad to the west, and to the east, and to the north, and to the south: and in thee and in thy seed shall all the families of the earth be blessed.

15And, behold, I am with thee, and will keep thee in all places whither thou goest, and will bring thee again into this land; for I will not leave thee, until I have done that which I have spoken to thee of.

13. The nation would become divided into two kingdoms

Bible passage: 1 Kings 11:29-33
Written: More than 2,500 years ago

After the 12 Tribes of Israel took control of the land of Canaan, about 3,400 years ago, the Israelites were governed by judges instead of kings. The reign of the judges lasted until about 3,000 years ago when a man named Saul became the first king of Israel. He was succeeded by King David, who in turn was succeeded by King Solomon. These kings ruled over a united kingdom that included all 12 Tribes of Israel.

In 1 Kings 11:29-33, however, a prophet named Ahijah prophesied that the united kingdom of Israel would break into two. Ahijah lived about 2,900 years ago, when Solomon, the son of David, ruled over the land of Israel.

Solomon, during his reign, had turned away from God, as did many other people. Ahijah prophesied that because of this unfaithfulness, the united kingdom would break up.

After Solomon died, his son, Rehoboam, became king, and the northern part of the land of Israel broke away and formed a new kingdom. That kingdom retained the name of Israel and consisted of 10 of the 12 Tribes of Israel. Jeroboam served as their king.

The southern part of the land of Israel, which included the city of Jerusalem and the Temple, became known as the kingdom of Judah. This kingdom was dominated by Israelites from the tribe of Judah, although there also were Israelites from other tribes living there.

- - -

Here is 1 Kings 11:29-33 (KJV):

29 And it came to pass at that time when Jeroboam went out

of Jerusalem, that the prophet Ahijah the Shilonite found him in the way; and he had clad himself with a new garment; and they two were alone in the field:

30 And Ahijah caught the new garment that was on him, and rent it in twelve pieces:

31 And he said to Jeroboam, Take thee ten pieces: for thus saith the LORD, the God of Israel, Behold, I will rend the kingdom out of the hand of Solomon, and will give ten tribes to thee:

32 (But he shall have one tribe for my servant David's sake, and for Jerusalem's sake, the city which I have chosen out of all the tribes of Israel:)

33 Because that they have forsaken me, and have worshipped Ashtoreth the goddess of the Zidonians, Chemosh the god of the Moabites, and Milcom the god of the children of Ammon, and have not walked in my ways, to do that which is right in mine eyes, and to keep my statutes and my judgments, as did David his father.

14. The northern kingdom of Israel would be conquered

Bible passage: Isaiah 7:7,8
Written: About 2,700 years ago

After the land of Israel had been divided into two kingdoms, the two often were in conflict with one another.

About 2,700 years ago, the people of Judah were being threatened by an alliance involving the country of Aram (Syria) and the northern kingdom of Israel. That conflict is described in the seventh chapter of the Old Testament book of Isaiah.

In Isaiah 7:7, the prophet informed the people of Judah that the alliance would fail in its plans against Judah. And, in the next verse, Isaiah prophesied that the northern kingdom of Israel would come to an end, and that its inhabitants would become broken as a people.

The Assyrians later invaded and conquered the northern kingdom, in about 722 BC. Afterwards, they transplanted some of the northern Israelites and replaced them with foreigners plucked from other regions of the Assyrian empire. Some examples of this are referenced in Ezra 4:2 and 2 Kings 17:24.

Josephus, a Jewish historian who lived during the first century of this era, also wrote about the transplanting of people in the northern part of the land of Israel:

> But the king of Assyria, whose name was Tiglath-Pileser, when he had made an expedition against the Israelites, and had overrun all the land of Gilead, and the region beyond Jordan, and the adjoining country, which is called Galilee, and Kadesh, and Hazor, he made the inhabitants prisoners, and transplanted them into his own kingdom.
> - Josephus, *Antiquities of the Jews,* Book IX, Chapter 11, as translated by William Whiston.

The northern kingdom of Israel, which the Bible sometimes refers to as Ephraim, never recovered from the destruction brought upon it by the Assyrians. And, the people of the northern kingdom were shattered as a people, losing their identity as distinct tribes of Israel.

- - -

Here is Isaiah 7:7,8 (KJV):

7 Thus saith the Lord GOD, It shall not stand, neither shall it come to pass.

8 For the head of Syria is Damascus, and the head of Damascus is Rezin; and within threescore and five years shall Ephraim be broken, that it be not a people.

15. The southern kingdom of Judah would be conquered

Bible passage: Isaiah 39:5-7
Written: About 2,700 years ago

The southern kingdom of Judah, unlike the northern kingdom of Israel, survived the wrath and aspirations of the Assyrian Empire. But, a new empire would rise up from Babylon and conquer the Assyrians, as well as the people of Judah.

Isaiah, who had prophesied about the destruction of the northern kingdom of Israel, also foretold the conquest of Judah. In Isaiah 39:5-7, the prophet informed King Hezekiah of Judah that there would come a time when the Babylonians would loot and subdue Judah.

After the time of Isaiah, the Babylonians fought and conquered the Assyrians, about 2,600 years ago, and assumed control over a large swath of land that included much of the Middle East. Afterwards, the Babylonians began subjugating Judah. In about the year 605 BC, the Babylonians began taking some of the Jews from Judah as captives to Babylon. And, in 586 BC, the Babylonians destroyed the city of Jerusalem and the Temple.

Babylon dominated Judah until about 539 BC, when a coalition of Medes and Persians conquered Babylon. Afterwards, some Jews returned from exile and began a process of rebuilding and repopulating Jerusalem and the surrounding cities and towns.

- - -

Here is Isaiah 39:5-7 (KJV):

5 Then said Isaiah to Hezekiah, Hear the word of the LORD of hosts:

6 Behold, the days come, that all that is in thine house, and that which thy fathers have laid up in store until this day, shall be carried to Babylon: nothing shall be left, saith the LORD.

7 And of thy sons that shall issue from thee, which thou shalt beget, shall they take away; and they shall be eunuchs in the palace of the king of Babylon.

16. The prophet Jeremiah explained why Judah would be punished

Bible passage: Jeremiah 32:32-37
Written: About 2,600 years ago

Jeremiah, a Biblical prophet who lived about 2,600 years ago, warned the people of Judah about the cost of turning away from God and told them that they would be subjected to domination by Babylon.

In Jeremiah 32:32-37, and elsewhere in the book of Jeremiah, the prophet described the widespread corruption and contempt for God that existed during his time. Among other offenses, some people had built places of worship to honor a false god named Baal, and others had sacrificed their children to a false god named Molech.

Here is Jeremiah 32:32-37 (KJV):

32 Because of all the evil of the children of Israel and of the
children of Judah, which they have done to provoke me to
anger, they, their kings, their princes, their priests, and their
prophets, and the men of Judah, and the inhabitants of
Jerusalem.

33 And they have turned unto me the back, and not the face:
though I taught them, rising up early and teaching them, yet
they have not hearkened to receive instruction.

34 But they set their abominations in the house, which is
called by my name, to defile it.

35 And they built the high places of Baal, which are in the
valley of the son of Hinnom, to cause their sons and their
daughters to pass through the fire unto Molech; which I
commanded them not, neither came it into my mind, that
they should do this abomination, to cause Judah to sin.

36 And now therefore thus saith the LORD, the God of
Israel, concerning this city, whereof ye say, It shall be
delivered into the hand of the king of Babylon by the
sword, and by the famine, and by the pestilence;

37 Behold, I will gather them out of all countries, whither I
have driven them in mine anger, and in my fury, and in
great wrath; and I will bring them again unto this place, and
I will cause them to dwell safely:

17. **Jerusalem and the Temple would be destroyed**

Bible passage: Micah 3:11,12
Written: About 2,700 years ago

Micah lived about 2,700 years ago, about a century before the time of Jeremiah. Like Jeremiah, Micah forewarned his people that turning away from God would result in punishment, and that this punishment would involve Jerusalem. Micah provided bleak details in his prophecy:

> Therefore shall Zion for your sake be plowed as a field, and Jerusalem shall become heaps, and the mountain of the house as the high places of the forest. (Micah 3:12, KJV)

The prophecy was fulfilled during ancient times. The Babylonians destroyed Jerusalem and the Temple about 2,600 years ago, during a military invasion.

And the city was destroyed again, by the Romans, during the first and second centuries of this era, after the time of Christ.

The destructions and their severity have been recorded in a variety of ways:

• The destruction caused by the Babylonians is described in 2 Kings 25:8–21. There, we are told that a Babylonian commander set fire to the Temple and the royal palace, and that he burned down every important building in the city. The Babylonian army also broke down the walls around the city.

• Josephus, who witnessed the Roman destruction of

Jerusalem during the first century, wrote that even the foundations of the Temple were dug up. He described this in his book, *The Wars of the Jews,* Book VII, Chapter 8.

• Judaic literature records a literal plowing of all or part of Jerusalem, at the hands of the Romans. *The Babylonian Talmud,* which is a compilation of Judaism-related writings that was completed about 1,500 years ago, speaks of a plowing of Jerusalem, in Tract Taanith, Chapter 4. There, it mentions five calamities that are said to have happened on the ninth day of the Jewish month of Ab, with the fifth calamity being the plowing of Jerusalem.

- - -

Here is Micah 3:11,12 (KJV):

11The heads thereof judge for reward, and the priests thereof teach for hire, and the prophets thereof divine for money: yet will they lean upon the LORD, and say, Is not the LORD among us? none evil can come upon us.

12Therefore shall Zion for your sake be plowed as a field, and Jerusalem shall become heaps, and the mountain of the house as the high places of the forest.

18. Judah would survive the Babylonian domination

Bible passage: Jeremiah 24:4-7
Written: About 2,600 years ago

In Jeremiah 24:4-7, Jeremiah received a prophecy from God about the future of the Jewish community that had been forced into exile in Babylon ("the land of the Chaldeans"). In this prophecy, God promised to protect the exiles, to preserve them, and to bring them back to their homeland.

Whereas the northern tribes of Israel lost their identity as distinct tribes after they were conquered by the Assyrians, the southern tribe of Judah would survive its time in exile, with its identity intact.

- - -

Here is Jeremiah 24:4-7 (KJV):

4 Again the word of the LORD came unto me, saying,

5 Thus saith the LORD, the God of Israel; Like these good figs, so will I acknowledge them that are carried away captive of Judah, whom I have sent out of this place into the land of the Chaldeans for their good.

6 For I will set mine eyes upon them for good, and I will bring them again to this land: and I will build them, and not pull them down; and I will plant them, and not pluck them up.

7 And I will give them an heart to know me, that I am the LORD: and they shall be my people, and I will be their God: for they shall return unto me with their whole heart.

19. Judah would return from exile

Bible passage: Jeremiah 29:10
Written: About 2,600 years ago

In Jeremiah 29:10, the people of Judah were told that their punishment at the hands of the Babylonians would be temporary, that it would come to an end, and that the exiles would be brought back to their homeland.

Seventy years after Babylon rose to power, its empire was stripped from its hands by Cyrus, in 539 BC, who led a coalition of Medes and Persians. Cyrus later issued a decree, releasing the exiles and giving them the freedom to leave Babylon to return to Judah.

Details about the return to Judah are recorded in the Bible's books of Ezra and Nehemiah.

- - -

Here is Jeremiah 29:10 (NIV):

This is what the LORD says: "When seventy years are completed for Babylon, I will come to you and fulfill my gracious promise to bring you back to this place."

20. **Jerusalem would be rebuilt**

Bible passage: Daniel 9:24-25
Written: Daniel lived more than 2,500 years ago

Daniel, another prophet from the Old Testament era, was among a group of people from Judah taken to Babylon as captives, sometime around 605 BC. About 20 years later, in 586 BC, the Babylonians destroyed Jerusalem and the Temple, turning Daniel's homeland into a land of ruins.

In the later part of his life, after the fall of Babylon, Daniel prayed to God on behalf of his people.

The response that he received is recorded in the ninth chapter of the book of Daniel. There, among other things, Daniel is told that the city of Jerusalem would be rebuilt.

After the fall of Babylon, some of the exiled Jews returned

to Jerusalem and began rebuilding the city. The process was not without difficulty. As explained in the book of Nehemiah, the returning Jews were met with hostility from other groups of people in the area. Even so, the Jews succeeded in rebuilding the walls around the city in a short amount of time. Afterwards, other parts of the city were restored.

Daniel's prophecy, however, went beyond the reconstruction of a fallen city. As indicated in Daniel 9:25, the Messiah would appear sometime after the rebuilding of Jerusalem.

- - -

Here is Daniel 9:24-25 (KJV):

24Seventy weeks are determined upon thy people and upon thy holy city, to finish the transgression, and to make an end of sins, and to make reconciliation for iniquity, and to bring in everlasting righteousness, and to seal up the vision and prophecy, and to anoint the most Holy.

25Know therefore and understand, that from the going forth of the commandment to restore and to build Jerusalem unto the Messiah the Prince shall be seven weeks, and threescore and two weeks: the street shall be built again, and the wall, even in troublous times.

Chapter 3
10 prophecies fulfilled by Jesus' birth

The Old Testament of the Bible was written before the time of Jesus. It contains many prophecies about a Messiah, someone who would suffer and die for the sins of others and reign forever as king. The Old Testament was written over a period of time that lasted as many as a thousand years, from the time of Moses, about 3,400 years ago, through the time of Malachi, about 2,400 years ago. The prophetic revelations accumulated over that time, creating a progressively detailed portrait of the Messiah. The 10 prophecies selected for review in this chapter involve the lineage and birth of the Messiah.

21. A worldwide blessing [the Messiah] would come from Abraham

Bible passage: Genesis 22:18
Written: As early as 1400 BC, about 3,400 years ago

The Bible's book of Genesis, among other things, contains prophecies about a Messiah. Some of those prophecies foretold details about his lineage.

In Genesis 22:18, for example, there is a prophecy that the nations of the world would be blessed through Abraham's "seed," or "offspring," depending on the English translation of the underlying Hebrew word:

> And in thy seed shall all the nations of the earth be blessed; because thou hast obeyed my voice. (Genesis 22:18, KJV)

As explained in later verses of the Bible, the prophetic promise of a worldwide blessing is handed down from Abraham to some of his specifically named descendants. At times, details are added, and it becomes clearer that the promise ultimately involves the Messiah.

22. A worldwide blessing [the Messiah] would come from Isaac

Bible passage: Genesis 26:1-5
Written: As early as 1400 BC, about 3,400 years ago

In Genesis 26:1-5, it was revealed that a promise that God had made previously to Abraham would be fulfilled though Abraham's son Isaac.

Abraham had children with more than one woman. But, in these verses of Genesis, it was revealed that it would be Isaac, who was Abraham's only child through his wife, Sarah, who would be Abraham's descendant through whom all nations on earth would be blessed.

- - -

Here is Genesis 26:1-5 (KJV):

1And there was a famine in the land, beside the first famine that was in the days of Abraham. And Isaac went unto Abimelech king of the Philistines unto Gerar.

2And the LORD appeared unto him, and said, Go not down into Egypt; dwell in the land which I shall tell thee of:

3Sojourn in this land, and I will be with thee, and will bless thee; for unto thee, and unto thy seed, I will give all these countries, and I will perform the oath which I sware unto Abraham thy father;

4And I will make thy seed to multiply as the stars of heaven, and will give unto thy seed all these countries; and in thy seed shall all the nations of the earth be blessed;

5Because that Abraham obeyed my voice, and kept my charge, my commandments, my statutes, and my laws.

23. **A worldwide blessing [the Messiah] would come from Jacob**

Bible passage: Genesis 28:13,14
Written: As early as 1400 BC, about 3,400 years ago

In Genesis 28:13,14, it was revealed that the world would be blessed through Jacob's offspring:

> And, behold, the LORD stood above it, and said, I am the LORD God of Abraham thy father, and the God of Isaac: the land whereon thou liest, to thee will I give it, and to thy seed; And thy seed shall be as the dust of the earth, and thou shalt spread abroad to the west, and to the east, and to the north, and to the south: and in thee and in thy seed shall all the families of the earth be blessed. (Genesis 28:13,14, KJV)

In earlier verses of Genesis, this promise was given to Abraham. Later, it was revealed that it would be fulfilled through Abraham's son Isaac. And in these verses, it was revealed that it would be fulfilled through Isaac's son Jacob.

In other words, God decided that the world would be

blessed through Abraham's "offspring" or "seed" through his son Isaac and grandson Jacob, rather than through any of Abraham's other children or grandchildren.

Jacob, whose name was later changed to Israel, became the father of the patriarchs of the 12 Tribes of Israel. Jacob lived about 4,000 years ago, which is about 2,000 years before the time of Jesus.

24. The Messiah would be a descendant of Jesse

Bible passage: Isaiah 11:1-10
Written: About 2,700 years ago

The prophecy in Isaiah 11:1-10, among other things, affirmed that the Messiah would be a descendant of Jesse, who was King David's father. Isaiah's prophecy also echoed a sentiment found in other prophecies, that the Messiah would have an impact on people beyond the land of Israel.

This sentiment was recognized and commented upon by early Christian writers outside of the Bible. As explained by Justin Martyr, a Christian writer who lived during the second century of this era:

> And Isaiah, another prophet, foretelling the same things in other words, spoke thus : "A star shall rise out of Jacob, and a flower shall spring from the root of Jesse; and His arm shall the nations trust."
> - *The First Apology of Justin,* Chapter XXXII.

Jesus is recorded as being a descendant of Jesse in the New Testament books of Matthew and Luke.

\- - -

Here is Isaiah 11:1-10 (KJV):

1And there shall come forth a rod out of the stem of Jesse,
and a Branch shall grow out of his roots:

2And the spirit of the LORD shall rest upon him, the spirit
of wisdom and understanding, the spirit of counsel and
might, the spirit of knowledge and of the fear of the LORD;

3And shall make him of quick understanding in the fear of
the LORD: and he shall not judge after the sight of his
eyes, neither reprove after the hearing of his ears:

4But with righteousness shall he judge the poor, and
reprove with equity for the meek of the earth: and he shall
smite the earth: with the rod of his mouth, and with the
breath of his lips shall he slay the wicked.

5And righteousness shall be the girdle of his loins, and
faithfulness the girdle of his reins.

6The wolf also shall dwell with the lamb, and the leopard
shall lie down with the kid; and the calf and the young lion
and the fatling together; and a little child shall lead them.

7And the cow and the bear shall feed; their young ones
shall lie down together: and the lion shall eat straw like the
ox.

8And the sucking child shall play on the hole of the asp,
and the weaned child shall put his hand on the cockatrice'
den.

9They shall not hurt nor destroy in all my holy mountain:
for the earth shall be full of the knowledge of the LORD, as
the waters cover the sea.

10And in that day there shall be a root of Jesse, which shall stand for an ensign of the people; to it shall the Gentiles seek: and his rest shall be glorious.

25. **The Messiah would be a descendant of King David**

Bible passage: Jeremiah 23:5
Written: About 2,600 years ago

During ancient times, Jews often referred to the promised Messiah as the "son of David," meaning he was to be a descendant of King David.

One of the prophecies revealing that the Messiah would be a descendant of David can be found in Jeremiah 23:5. There, the prophet spoke of a time when a "branch" of David, which in this context means a descendant of David, would rise up and rule with true righteousness and justice.

This is similar to the phrasing used in Isaiah 11:1, which is part of a prophecy that, among other things, showed that the Messiah would be a descendant of Jesse, who was David's father.

King David lived about 3,000 years ago. He was Israel's second king, but he was the first of many kings from the Tribe of Judah. Jeremiah lived about 2,600 years ago, about 600 years before Jesus arrived and announced that he was the Messiah.

In the New Testament of the Bible, Jesus is recorded as being a descendant of King David, as well as David's father, Jesse, and other ancestors, including Judah, Jacob, Isaac, and Abraham. The genealogy listed in Matthew 1:1-

17 shows Jesus' ancestors through his adoptive father, Joseph. The genealogy in Luke 3:23-38 also includes David, Jesse, Judah, Jacob, Isaac, and Abraham. Some scholars believe that the genealogy in the book of Luke shows Jesus' ancestors through his mother, Mary.

- - -

Here is Jeremiah 23:5 (KJV):

Behold, the days come, saith the LORD, that I will raise unto David a righteous Branch, and a King shall reign and prosper, and shall execute judgment and justice in the earth.

26. Isaiah foreshadowed the virgin birth of Jesus

Bible passage: Isaiah 7:13,14
Written: About 2,700 years ago

In Isaiah 7, the prophet Isaiah delivered a long prophecy that involved the future of Judah and the "house of David," which is a phrase that refers to the descendants of King David. In Isaiah 7:13,14, the prophet specifically addressed the house of David:

> And he said, Hear ye now, O house of David; Is it a small thing for you to weary men, but will ye weary my God also? Therefore the Lord himself shall give you a sign; Behold, a virgin shall conceive, and bear a son, and shall call his name Immanuel. (Isaiah 7:13,14, KJV)

In these verses of Isaiah, the prophet was informing the descendants of King David that God himself would give them a sign: A virgin would conceive and give birth to a son, and the son would be called Immanuel, which in

Hebrew means "God with us" or "God is with us."

As explained in the New Testament, the Messiah, Jesus, who was born about 700 years later, was conceived by the Holy Spirit and born of the virgin Mary. Jesus is fully human and fully God. As such, he can be called, in the fullest and most literal sense, "God with us."

Two of the Gospels in the New Testament describe the circumstances involving the birth of Jesus and both testify that Jesus was born of a virgin (Matthew 1:18-25 and Luke 1:26-38). Both of these Gospels also record that Jesus is a descendant of King David.

The Hebrew word in Isaiah 7:14 that is being translated into English as "virgin," is the Hebrew word *alma.* Some commentators have claimed that the word should be translated as "maiden" or "young woman." But, in addition to the fact that maidens were religiously and culturally expected to be virgins until marriage, the word *alma* is used elsewhere in the Bible in reference to virgins.

According to one scholarly work: "There is no instance where it can be proved that *'almâ* designates a young woman who is not a virgin. The fact of virginity is obvious in Gen 24:43 where *'almâ* is used of one who was being sought as a bride for Isaac." - R. Laird Harris, et al, *Theological Wordbook of the Old Testament.*

27. The Messiah would be born in Bethlehem

Bible passage: Micah 5:2
Written: About 2,700 years ago

In Micah 5:2, there is a prophecy that revealed that Bethlehem would be the birthplace of the Messiah:

> But thou, Bethlehem Ephratah, though thou be little among the thousands of Judah, yet out of thee shall he come forth unto me that is to be ruler in Israel; whose goings forth have been from of old, from everlasting. (Micah 5;2, KJV)

The prophecy, which was written about 700 years before the birth of Jesus, is effective in a simple way: It eliminates all other cities and towns throughout the world as a place in which the Messiah would be born. It narrows the possibilities to one tiny village, near Jerusalem.

And throughout the span of the past 27 centuries, since the time of the prophet Micah, Bethlehem is credited as being the birthplace for the only person who is widely accepted as being the Messiah, by people throughout the world, and that person is Jesus Christ.

28. The Messiah would appear after a succession of rulers from the Tribe of Judah

Bible passage: Genesis 49:10
Written: As early as 1400 BC, about 3,400 years ago

In Genesis 49, there is a passage that many commentators throughout the ages have regarded as being a prophecy about the timing of the arrival of the Messiah:

> The sceptre shall not depart from Judah, nor a lawgiver from between his feet, until Shiloh come; and unto him shall the gathering of the people be. (Genesis 49:10, KJV)

The Hebrew word that is rendered as *Shiloh* in the KJV English translation is sometimes translated in other ways. The NIV English translators, for example, use the word *he.* Regardless of how the word is rendered into English, Christian and non-Christian commentators have traditionally regarded the passage as Messianic.

Justin Martyr, a Christian writer who lived during the second century of this era, described this prophecy as meaning that the descendants of Judah were to have a continuity of rulers and lawgivers until the Messiah arrived:

> It is yours to make accurate inquiry, and ascertain up to whose time the Jews had a lawgiver and king of their own. Up to the time of Jesus Christ, who taught us, and interpreted the prophecies which were not yet understood, [they had a lawgiver] as was foretold by the holy and divine Spirit of prophecy through Moses, "that a ruler would not fail the Jews until He should come for whom the kingdom was reserved" (for Judah was the forefather of the Jews, from whom also they have their name of Jews);
> - Justin Martyr, *The First Apology of Justin,* Chapter XXXII.

Some commentators have suggested that the Jews had a continuous succession of rulers, in various forms, whether as kings or as governors, etc., from the days of King David through the time of Jesus, and that this continuity was broken during the time of Jesus. Martin Luther, for example, suggested in his writings that it was the reign of King Herod, an Idumean who had been appointed by the Romans to govern the Jews, that marked the break in the continuity of rulers.

And, as Justin mentioned in his writings, the Jews lost all forms of civil government during the century in which

Jesus lived. About 40 years after the crucifixion of Jesus, the Romans completely destroyed Jerusalem, the Temple, and many towns throughout the land of Israel. The Romans also forced many Jews out of their homeland and into exile.

Non-Christian sources of commentary also have regarded Genesis 49:10 as being Messianic. In the Talmud, for example, the word *Shiloh* is seen as a reference to the Messiah:

> R. Johanan said: For the sake of the Messiah. What is his [the Messiah's] name? — The School of R. Shila said: His name is Shiloh, for it is written, until Shiloh come.
> - *Babylonian Talmud,* Tract Sanhedrin, Chapter XI, as translated by H. Freedman.

The Talmud is a collection of Judaic writings that were compiled in written form beginning sometime after the first century of this era.

29. The Messiah would appear after the rebuilding of Jerusalem

Bible passage: Daniel 9:25
Written: Daniel lived more than 2,500 years ago

The prophecy in Daniel 9:24-27 provided many insights about events that would happen after the fall of the Babylonian Empire, about 2,500 years ago. Among those insights was the detail that the Messiah would appear after the rebuilding of the city of Jerusalem:

> Know therefore and understand, that from the going forth of the commandment to restore and to build Jerusalem unto the Messiah the Prince shall be seven weeks, and threescore and two weeks: the street shall

> be built again, and the wall, even in troublous times. (Daniel 9:25, KJV)

Jerusalem had been destroyed by the Babylonians in 586 BC and was in ruins for most of Daniel's life. The prophecy revealed that the city would be rebuilt again, and that afterwards the Messiah would appear.

These details coincide with the circumstances of the arrival of Jesus as the Messiah about 2,000 years ago. By that time, the city had been resettled and rebuilt.

30. The Messiah would appear before the (Roman) destruction of Jerusalem

Bible passage: Daniel 9:26
Written: Daniel lived more than 2,500 years ago

Whereas Daniel 9:25 said that the Messiah would arrive after the rebuilding of Jerusalem, the next verse showed that the arrival would take place before the city would be destroyed again:

> And after threescore and two weeks shall Messiah be cut off, but not for himself: and the people of the prince that shall come shall destroy the city and the sanctuary; and the end thereof shall be with a flood, and unto the end of the war desolations are determined. (Daniel 9:26, KJV)

This, too, corresponds to the timing of Jesus' arrival as the Messiah about 2,000 years ago. About 40 years after Jesus was crucified, the Romans destroyed Jerusalem. The destruction was so complete that some of the effects remain visible today.

Chapter 4
10 prophecies fulfilled during Jesus' life and ministry

The 10 Bible prophecies selected for review in this chapter foretold important events involving the life and ministry of Jesus Christ, who lived about 2,000 years ago in the land of Israel.

31. A messenger would prepare the way for the Lord

Bible passage: Malachi 3:1
Written: About 2,400 years ago

In Malachi 3:1, the prophet, who lived about 2,400 years ago, foretold of a messenger who would prepare the way for the Lord:

> Behold, I will send my messenger, and he shall prepare the way before me: and the LORD, whom ye seek, shall suddenly come to his temple, even the messenger of the covenant, whom ye delight in: behold, he shall come, saith the LORD of hosts. (Malachi 3:1, KJV)

About 400 years later, as described in Matthew 11:10, Jesus proclaimed that John the Baptist was the messenger who had been prophesied beforehand.

John the Baptist helped prepare people for the ministry of

Jesus. In fact, he announced that Jesus is the Son of God, and he proclaimed that Jesus is the lamb of God who takes away the sin of the world:

> The next day John seeth Jesus coming unto him, and saith, Behold the Lamb of God, which taketh away the sin of the world. This is he of whom I said, After me cometh a man which is preferred before me: for he was before me. And I knew him not: but that he should be made manifest to Israel, therefore am I come baptizing with water. And John bare record, saying, I saw the Spirit descending from heaven like a dove, and it abode upon him. And I knew him not: but he that sent me to baptize with water, the same said unto me, Upon whom thou shalt see the Spirit descending, and remaining on him, the same is he which baptizeth with the Holy Ghost. And I saw, and bare record that this is the Son of God. (John 1:29-34, KJV)

The death of John the Baptist is recorded in Matthew 14:1-12; Mark 6:14-29; and Luke 9:1-9. He was beheaded in about the year 30 AD, by Herod (Antipas), who was one of the sons of King Herod.

His death also was recorded by Josephus, a first-century Jewish historian, who wrote:

> Now some of the Jews thought that the destruction of Herod's army came from God, and that very justly, as a punishment of what he did against John, that was called the *Baptist ;* for Herod slew him, who was a good man, and commanded the Jews to exercise virtue, both as to righteousness towards one another, and piety towards God, and so to come to baptism ; . . .
> - Josephus, *Antiquities of the Jews,* Book XVIII, Chapter 5, as translated by William Whiston.

32. **The ministry of Jesus is foreshadowed by Isaiah**

Bible passage: Isaiah 61:1,2
Written: About 2,700 years ago

During his ministry about 2,000 years ago, Jesus returned to the town of Nazareth, where he grew up, and attended a service at a synagogue. During the service, as was customary, an attending person would read a selection of (Old Testament) scripture. On this occasion, it was Jesus who did the reading, and he read a passage from the scroll of Isaiah:

> The Spirit of the Lord GOD is upon me; because the LORD hath anointed me to preach good tidings unto the meek; he hath sent me to bind up the brokenhearted, to proclaim liberty to the captives, and the opening of the prison to them that are bound; To proclaim the acceptable year of the LORD, (Isaiah 61:1,2a, KJV)

When he stopped reading, he rolled up the scroll, sat down and said, "Today this scripture is fulfilled in your hearing" (Luke 4:21, NIV). The event is described in Luke 4:14-21.

The words found in Isaiah 61:1,2a help to explain the nature of Jesus' ministry about 2,000 years ago, as he taught people about the gift of salvation and eternal life with God.

And, the portion of Isaiah 61:2 that Jesus did not read is understood by many Christian commentators, including Irenaeus, to be a reference to another role that Jesus will fulfill, in the future, when he returns to judge the living and the dead.

Irenaeus is a Christian who lived during the second century of this era. Irenaeus' comments involving Jesus and Isaiah 61:1,2 can be found in his work, *Against Heresies,* Book II, Chapter 22.

In that chapter, Irenaeus characterized the "the acceptable year of the Lord" as being "This present time, therefore, in which men are called and saved by the Lord . . . "

And, Irenaeus wrote that the day of vengeance, which is alluded to later in verse 2, refers to judgment day.

- - -

Here is Isaiah 61:1,2 (KJV):

1The Spirit of the Lord GOD is upon me; because the LORD hath anointed me to preach good tidings unto the meek; he hath sent me to bind up the brokenhearted, to proclaim liberty to the captives, and the opening of the prison to them that are bound;

2To proclaim the acceptable year of the LORD, and the day of vengeance of our God; to comfort all that mourn;

33. **He would perform miracles**

Bible passage: Isaiah 35:4-6
Written: About 2,700 years ago

Centuries before Jesus began performing miracles in the land of Israel, the prophet Isaiah spoke of someone opening the eyes of the blind and the ears of the deaf:

> Say to them that are of a fearful heart, Be strong, fear not: behold, your God will come with vengeance, even

> God with a recompence; he will come and save you. Then the eyes of the blind shall be opened, and the ears of the deaf shall be unstopped. Then shall the lame man leap as an hart, and the tongue of the dumb sing: for in the wilderness shall waters break out, and streams in the desert. (Isaiah 35:4-6, KJV)
>
> Note: the word *dumb* in this context means *mute.*

Aside from spiritually healing people, Jesus also performed miracles of physical healing. The New Testament records dozens of miracles that Jesus performed during his ministry about 2,000 years ago, including healing people of blindness, deafness, muteness, and lameness. Examples can be found in Matthew 9:27-31; Mark 7:31-37; Luke 11:14; and John 5:5-17.

Jesus also performed other kinds of miracles, such as the calming of a storm (Luke 8:22-25), walking on water (Matthew 14:22-33), miraculously feeding thousands of people with a few handfuls of food (John 6:5-14), and bringing Jairus' daughter back to life (Luke 8:41,42, 49-56), and bringing Lazarus back to life (John 11:1-44).

34. **God promised another prophet like Moses**

Bible passage: Deuteronomy 18:15-18
Written: As early as 1400 BC, about 3,400 years ago

In Deuteronomy 18:15-18, Moses told the Israelites that God would raise up another prophet like Moses.

After the time of Moses, God raised up a succession of prophets, including Isaiah, Jeremiah, Ezekiel, Daniel, and Jesus. Like Moses, Jesus combined the offices of prophet, priest, leader, and deliverer. None of the other prophets combined all of those functions.

Jesus and Moses share much else in common. Here are some examples:

• Both were delivered from the threat of death as infants. During the time of Moses' birth, the Pharaoh of Egypt commanded that all Hebrew male infants be killed, because he feared that the growing Hebrew population would become a threat to his power (Exodus 1:1-22; Exodus 2:1-10). During the time of Jesus' infancy, King Herod ordered the death of male infants in Bethlehem, because he feared that one of them (Jesus) would be regarded as king instead of Herod (Matthew 2:1-16).

• Both were born during times when the people of Israel were being oppressed. During Moses' time, the people of Israel were living in Egypt, where they were being oppressed and enslaved (Exodus 1:1-22). During Jesus' time, the people of Israel were oppressed by the Romans, who ruled over a vast empire that included the land of Israel.

• Both were adopted. Moses was adopted into the Pharaoh's household (Exodus 2:1-10). Jesus was adopted by Joseph (Matthew 1:18-24).

• Both performed miracles. One example for Moses can be found in Exodus 14:21, and one example for Jesus is recorded in Matthew 8:23–27.

• Both spent part of their lives in Egypt. Moses was born in Egypt because his forefathers had left Israel during a time of famine to seek refuge in Egypt. Jesus, as an infant, was taken to Egypt for a while because his life was being threatened within the land of Israel, by King Herod.

• Both interceded with God. Moses tried to offer himself as payment for the sins of the Israelites (Exodus 32:30-33). Jesus willingly died for our sins (Romans 5:7-9; 1 Corinthians 15:3; Hebrews 9:15; etc).

Although there are many similarities, there also are important differences. Jesus is fully human and fully God. And Jesus is the mediator between man and God:

> For there is one God, and one mediator between God and men, the man Christ Jesus; (1 Timothy 2:5, KJV)

- - -

Here is Deuteronomy 18:15-18 (KJV):

15The LORD thy God will raise up unto thee a Prophet from the midst of thee, of thy brethren, like unto me; unto him ye shall hearken;

16According to all that thou desiredst of the LORD thy God in Horeb in the day of the assembly, saying, Let me not hear again the voice of the LORD my God, neither let me see this great fire any more, that I die not.

17And the LORD said unto me, They have well spoken that which they have spoken.

18I will raise them up a Prophet from among their brethren, like unto thee, and will put my words in his mouth; and he shall speak unto them all that I shall command him.

35. The Messiah would enter Jerusalem while riding on a donkey

Bible passage: Zechariah 9:9
Written: About 2,500 years ago

In Zechariah 9:9, Zechariah gave a prophecy, one that has long since been regarded as Messianic, about a king arriving in Jerusalem in a humble way, by riding on a donkey.

About 500 years later, Jesus rode into Jerusalem on a donkey, as explained in Matthew 21:1-11; Mark 11:1-11; Luke 19:28-38; and John 12:12-19. The Gospels contain details that indicate that at least some of the people who witnessed the event understood the significance of what Jesus was doing.

In the Gospel of Matthew, for example, people are recorded as crying out, "Hosanna to the son of David:"

> And a very great multitude spread their garments in the way; others cut down branches from the trees, and strawed them in the way. And the multitudes that went before, and that followed, cried, saying, Hosanna to the son of David: Blessed is he that cometh in the name of the Lord; Hosanna in the highest. (Matthew 21:8,9, KJV).

The phrase, "son of David," is a Biblical way of referring to the promised Messiah, who was to be a descendant of King David.

In the Gospel of John, people also are recorded as crying out, "Blessed is the King of Israel that cometh in the name of the Lord:"

> On the next day much people that were come to the feast, when they heard that Jesus was coming to Jerusalem, Took branches of palm trees, and went forth to meet him, and cried, Hosanna: Blessed is the

> King of Israel that cometh in the name of the Lord.
> (John 12:12,13, KJV)

Matthew and John refer to the prophecy in Zechariah 9:9 in their description of the Jesus' entry into Jerusalem.

Zechariah 9:9 has been understood since ancient times as being a prophecy about the Messiah. This is attested to by a variety of scholars, including Alfred Edersheim, a Christian Jew who lived during the 1800s. Edersheim, who studied ancient Jewish writings, explained:

> The Messianic application of this verse in all its parts has already been repeatedly indicated. We may here add that there are many traditions about this donkey on which the Messiah is to ride; and so firm was the belief in it, that, according to the Talmud, 'if anyone saw a donkey in his dreams, he will see salvation' (Ber 56 b).
> - Edersheim, *The Life and Times of Jesus the Messiah.*

The Talmud offers additional commentary in which some Rabbis offered their opinions about how to reconcile various prophecies involving the timing of the Messiah and the manner in which he was to arrive. They noted that Zechariah announced that the Messiah would arrive humbly on a donkey and that Daniel prophesied that the Messiah would arrive in a very different way:

> R. Alexandri said: Jehoshua b. Levi propounded a contradiction: It reads [ibid. ix. 22]: 'I the Lord will hasten it in its time.' 'Hasten' and 'in its time' contradict each other. And the answer was that if they will be worthy I will hasten it, and if not, they must wait till the right time will come. The same said again that the same authority propounded another contradiction from [Dan. vii. 13]: 'Behold with the clouds of heaven came one like a son of man . . . ' [Zech. ix. 9]: 'Lowly and

> riding upon an ass.' And the answer was, if they will be worthy he will come with the clouds of heaven, and if not, he will come upon an ass.
> - *Babylonian Talmud,* Tract Sanhedrin, Chapter XI, as translated by Michael L. Rodkinson.

As reflected in this part of the Talmud, there was a sense of puzzlement as to how one Messiah could arrive in two different ways. And, the solution that is being proposed in this part of the Talmud - that the Messiah's means of arrival would depend on the worthiness of people - is not found in Biblical scripture.

Christians, however, believe that there is one Messiah who is to arrive twice, fulfilling the prophecies of both Zechariah and Daniel. Jesus arrived about 2,000 years ago and announced that he was the Messiah, in part by riding a donkey into Jerusalem. And he is to return in the future, in the manner described by Daniel, when he will judge the living and the dead.

- - -

Here is Zechariah 9:9 (KJV):

Rejoice greatly, O daughter of Zion; shout, O daughter of Jerusalem: behold, thy King cometh unto thee: he is just, and having salvation; lowly, and riding upon an ass, and upon a colt the foal of an ass.

36. Israel's history foreshadowed the life of the Messiah

Bible passage: Hosea 11:1
Written: Hosea lived about 2,800 years ago

In the book of Matthew, the author provided examples as to

how important events in the history of Israel are reflected in the life of Jesus.

One example that Matthew provided is found in Matthew 2:15, which alludes to another Bible passage, one that was written centuries beforehand:

> When Israel was a child, then I loved him, and called my son out of Egypt. (Hosea 11:1, KJV)

During ancient times, when the nation of Israel was in its infancy, the Israelites left their homeland, which had been struck by faminc. Escaping the threat of death, they migrated to Egypt. Generations later, the Israelites returned to the land of Israel.

When Jesus, who literally is the son of God, was an infant, Joseph and Mary took him to Egypt, to elude a threat of death from King Herod. After Herod's death, Jesus and his family returned to the land of Israel.

37. **The Messiah would appear in Galilee, be a light to Gentiles**

Bible passage: Isaiah 9:1,2
Written: About 2,700 years ago

In Matthew 4:12-17, Matthew wrote about a part of Jesus' public ministry that took place in Galilee. In doing so, Matthew cited an Old Testament passage found in the book of Isaiah:

> Nevertheless, there will be no more gloom for those who were in distress. In the past he humbled the land of Zebulun and the land of Naphtali, but in the future he will honor Galilee of the Gentiles, by the way of the sea, along the Jordan-

> The people walking in darkness
> have seen a great light;
> on those living in the land of the shadow of death
> a light has dawned. (Isaiah 9:1,2, NIV)

Although Jesus was born in Bethlehem, he was raised in Nazareth, which is a town in the northern part of the land of Israel, within the region of Galilee. Jesus also lived in Capernaum, which also is in Galilee, during part of his ministry. During the time of Jesus, Galilee was home to many Gentiles.

38. Isaiah spoke of a son who would be called God

Bible passage: Isaiah 9:6,7
Written: About 2,700 years ago

In Isaiah 9:6,7, which was written about 700 years before the time of Jesus, Isaiah prophesied that there would be a "son" who would be called "mighty God."

Isaiah also prophesied that this person would reign on the throne of King David and that his reign would be everlasting.

Christians acknowledge that Jesus is the fulfillment of this prophecy. Jesus is fully human and fully God, he is the "son" and he is the "mighty God." As a person, he is a descendant of King David (Luke 3:21-32). And, as God, Jesus is able to reign forever.

The teachings of Jesus, which are explained in the New Testament of the Bible, shape the lives of hundreds of millions of people throughout the world. The New Testament also says that Jesus will return in the future, to judge the living and the dead, and that his kingdom will have no end.

- - -

Here is Isaiah 9:6,7 (KJV):

6For unto us a child is born, unto us a son is given: and the government shall be upon his shoulder: and his name shall be called Wonderful, Counsellor, The mighty God, The everlasting Father, The Prince of Peace.

7Of the increase of his government and peace there shall be no end, upon the throne of David, and upon his kingdom, to order it, and to establish it with judgment and with justice from henceforth even for ever. The zeal of the LORD of hosts will perform this.

39. The Messiah would be rejected

Bible passage: Isaiah 53:1-4
Written: About 2,700 years ago

God gave the prophet Isaiah, who lived about seven centuries before the time of Jesus, many prophecies about the Messiah. Among them was a prophecy that the Messiah would be rejected. One example can be found in Isaiah 53:1-4.

Although Jesus was acknowledged as being the Messiah by some people, he was rejected by many others.

Jesus was rejected at various times during his ministry, including by people within the town of Nazareth, where he grew up, and by many religious leaders in Jerusalem, where he was crucified by the Romans.

The prophecy of rejection in Isaiah 53:1-4 is part of a broader prophecy that begins in Isaiah 52:13 and extends through Isaiah 53:12, which has been regarded as Messianic prophecy throughout history, even by non-Christian sources of commentary about the Bible.

In the Talmud, for example, which includes opinions from Rabbis about many Old Testament passages, a part of Isaiah 53, specifically Isaiah 53:4, is alluded to during a Rabbinic discussion about the Messiah:

> What is his [the Messiah's] name? . . . The Rabbis said: His name is 'the leper scholar,' as it is written, *Surely he hath borne our griefs, and carried our sorrows: yet we did esteem him a leper, smitten of God, and afflicted.*
> - *Babylonian Talmud,* Tract Sanhedrin, Chapter XI, as translated by H. Freedman.

The compilation of the Babylonian Talmud was completed sometime around the fifth or sixth century AD, about 1,500 years ago. Many other sources of commentary, throughout the centuries, also have described Isaiah 53 as being Messianic prophecy, including this example from a Rabbi named Moshe Alshekh, who lived during the 16th century:

> I may remark, then, that our Rabbis with one voice accept and affirm the opinion that the prophet is speaking of the King Messiah,
> - as quoted in *The Fifty-Third Chapter of Isaiah According to the Jewish Interpreters,* Volume II, Chapter XXXVII.

There also are other prophecies in the Bible that foretold that the Messiah would be rejected, including one found in Daniel 9:24-26.

Here is Isaiah 53:1-4 (KJV):

1Who hath believed our report? and to whom is the arm of the LORD revealed?

2For he shall grow up before him as a tender plant, and as a root out of a dry ground: he hath no form nor comeliness; and when we shall see him, there is no beauty that we should desire him.

3He is despised and rejected of men; a man of sorrows, and acquainted with grief: and we hid as it were our faces from him; he was despised, and we esteemed him not.

4Surely he hath borne our griefs, and carried our sorrows: yet we did esteem him stricken, smitten of God, and afflicted.

40. Daniel predicted when an anointed one (the Messiah) would be rejected

Bible passage: Daniel 9:24-26
Written: Daniel lived more than 2,500 years ago

The prophet Daniel lived more than 2,500 years ago, during a time when the Babylonians had destroyed Jerusalem and the Temple. He delivered a prophecy of what would happen afterwards. Part of that prophecy can be found in Daniel 9:24-26, which described a series of events that included the rejection of the Messiah:

1. First, there would be a decree to rebuild Jerusalem.

2. Then, Jerusalem would be rebuilt.

3. Then, an anointed one - the Messiah - would be "cut off," which is a phrase that is used in the Bible to refer to a rejection by means of separation, isolation, or death, etc. The phrase also is used in Isaiah 53:8, in regards to the Messiah:

> He was taken from prison and from judgment: and who shall declare his generation? for he was cut off out of the land of the living: for the transgression of my people was he stricken. (Isaiah 53:8, KJV)

4. And then, Jerusalem would be destroyed again.

These events later happened, in the same order in which they are described in Daniel 9:24-26:

1. After the Medes and Persians had conquered the Babylonians about 2,500 years ago, they assumed control of a large empire, which included the land of Israel. After the conquest, the Jews were given permission to rebuild Jerusalem, which was still in ruins after having been destroyed earlier by the Babylonians.

2. The Jews rebuilt Jerusalem and the Temple.

3. Then, about 2,000 years ago, Jesus announced that he is the Messiah. Many people rejected Jesus and he was executed by the Romans.

4. About 40 years after Jesus was executed, the Romans destroyed Jerusalem and the Temple.

- - -

Here is Daniel 9:24-26 (KJV):

24Seventy weeks are determined upon thy people and upon
thy holy city, to finish the transgression, and to make an
end of sins, and to make reconciliation for iniquity, and to
bring in everlasting righteousness, and to seal up the vision
and prophecy, and to anoint the most Holy.

25Know therefore and understand, that from the going forth
of the commandment to restore and to build Jerusalem unto
the Messiah the Prince shall be seven weeks, and threescore
and two weeks: the street shall be built again, and the wall,
even in troublous times.

26And after threescore and two weeks shall Messiah be cut
off, but not for himself: and the people of the prince that
shall come shall destroy the city and the sanctuary; and the
end thereof shall be with a flood, and unto the end of the
war desolations are determined.

Chapter 5
10 prophecies involving the betrayal, persecution and crucifixion of Jesus

These 10 prophecies are among many in the Bible that foreshadowed and foretold details involving the betrayal, persecution and crucifixion of Jesus Christ.

41. Jesus prophesied that he would be betrayed

Bible passage: Matthew 26:20,21
Written: During the first century AD, about 2,000 years ago

The Apostles of Jesus were in a unique position: They were able to see with their own eyes whether Jesus was the fulfillment of various Old Testament prophecies about the Messiah. And, they were able to see whether the prophecies that Jesus gave in regards to himself and his followers were being fulfilled.

Jesus prophesied, for example, that one of the 12 Apostles would betray him:

> Now when the even was come, he sat down with the twelve. And as they did eat, he said, Verily I say unto you, that one of you shall betray me. (Matthew 26:20,21, KJV)

A short time later, Judas Iscariot betrayed Jesus. The betrayal was followed by the arrest, trial, and execution of Jesus.

42. **Jesus prophesied that the Apostles would desert him**

Bible passage: Matthew 26:31,32
Written: During the first century AD, about 2,000 years ago

In Matthew 26:31,32, Jesus alluded to an Old Testament passage found in Zechariah 13:7 and prophesied that his Apostles soon would flee from him:

> Then Jesus told them, "This very night you will all fall away on account of me, for it is written:
>
> " 'I will strike the shepherd, and the sheep of the flock will be scattered.'
>
> But after I have risen, I will go ahead of you into Galilee." (Matthew 26:31,32, NIV)

Later, Judas Iscariot, who betrayed Jesus, led a crowd of armed people to the place where Jesus and some of his followers were staying. Jesus was arrested and the Apostles fled:

> Then all the disciples deserted him and fled. (Matthew 26:56b, NIV)

43. **Jesus prophesied that Peter would disown him**

Bible passage: Matthew 26:34
Written: During the first century AD, about 2,000 years

ago

After Jesus informed the Apostles, in Matthew 26, that they soon would abandon him, Peter responded that he would never abandon Jesus, even if everyone else did.

Jesus then specifically addressed Peter, prophesying that Peter would deny knowing Jesus:

> "I tell you the truth," Jesus answered, "this very night, before the rooster crows, you will disown me three times." (Matthew 26:34, NIV)

Soon after, Jesus was arrested and the Apostles scattered away from him. Later that night, as described in Matthew 26:69-75, Peter was approached by people who recognized him as an associate of Jesus. Peter denied what they said, claiming that he didn't know Jesus.

After Peter's denial, a rooster crowed, prompting Peter to remember the words that Jesus had spoken:

> Then he began to call down curses on himself and he swore to them, "I don't know the man!" Immediately a rooster crowed. Then Peter remembered the word Jesus had spoken: "Before the rooster crows, you will disown me three times." And he went outside and wept bitterly. (Matthew 26:74,75, NIV)

44. **Psalm 41 foreshadowed the betrayal of Jesus**

Bible passage: Psalm 41:9-12
Written: As early as about 1000 BC, about 3,000 years ago

In Psalm 41, the psalmist spoke of being betrayed by a

friend, someone close enough to have shared food with him (verse 9).

The psalms of the Bible were written before the time of Jesus, and many of them contain details that foreshadowed or foretold events in the life of Jesus, including his betrayal by a close friend.

As explained in Matthew 26:17-25 and Matthew 26:45-56, Jesus was betrayed by Judas Iscariot, who was one of the 12 Apostles, after sharing bread with him during the Last Supper. Later, Judas led a crowd of men armed with swords and clubs to the place where Jesus and some of his followers were staying, and Jesus was arrested. Jesus was executed a short time later.

- - -

Here is Psalm 41:9-12 (KJV):

9Yea, mine own familiar friend, in whom I trusted, which did eat of my bread, hath lifted up his heel against me.

10But thou, O LORD, be merciful unto me, and raise me up, that I may requite them.

11By this I know that thou favourest me, because mine enemy doth not triumph over me.

12And as for me, thou upholdest me in mine integrity, and settest me before thy face for ever.

45. **Psalms foreshadowed being hated without cause**

Bible passages: Psalm 35:19 and Psalm 69:4

Written: As early as about 1000 BC, about 3,000 years ago

Like many of the Bible's psalms, Psalms 35 and 69 offer details that foreshadowed events that later happened to Jesus Christ. Among them is the detail of being hated without cause:

> Let not them that are mine enemies wrongfully rejoice over me: neither let them wink with the eye that hate me without a cause. (Psalm 35:19, KJV)

> They that hate me without a cause are more than the hairs of mine head: they that would destroy me, being mine enemies wrongfully, are mighty: then I restored that which I took not away. (Psalm 69:4, KJV)

In John 15:24,25, Jesus spoke of being hated without cause, even though he had performed many miracles.

46. **Psalm 22 foreshadowed the crucifixion of Jesus**

Bible passage: Psalm 22:1-18
Written: As early as about 1000 BC, about 3,000 years ago

Psalm 22, which was written before the time of Jesus, contains many details that foreshadowed the crucifixion of Jesus.

Below is a partial list of details from the psalm, along with commentary as to how they foreshadowed events involving the crucifixion:

• In Psalm 22:16, the psalmist wrote of a man being encircled and having his hands and feet pierced, mauled, or attacked. During the crucifixion, Jesus was surrounded by enemies and his hands and feet were pierced with nails, as part of the crucifixion process. These events are described and alluded to in John 19:23-37; John 20:24-29; and Luke 24:37-40.

• The psalmist wrote of being mocked by an onlooker who said: "He trusted on the LORD that he would deliver him: let him deliver him, seeing he delighted in him" (Psalm 22:8, KJV). After Jesus had been nailed to the cross, he too was mocked for his trust in God: "He trusted in God; let him deliver him now, if he will have him: for he said, I am the Son of God" (Matthew 27:43, KJV).

• In Psalm 22:18, the psalmist wrote of onlookers gambling for pieces of clothing that belonged to the person being persecuted. As explained in Matthew 27:35, Roman soldiers gambled, by casting lots, for articles of clothing that had been removed from Jesus when he was being crucified.

Many Christian scholars have written about their views of the significance of Psalm 22 in regards to the crucifixion of Jesus. The late Charles Briggs, who had been a professor at the Union Theological Seminary, wrote the following in regards to Psalm 22:

> These sufferings transcend those of any historical sufferer, with the single exception of Jesus Christ. They find their exact counterpart in the sufferings of the cross. ... This ideal is a Messianic ideal, and finds its only historical realization in Jesus Christ.
> - Briggs, *Messianic Prophecy.*

In addition to the details in Psalm 22 that foreshadowed the crucifixion, it is worth noting that, in Matthew 27:46, Jesus is quoted as saying the same words that begin Psalm 22, after he had been nailed to the cross.

Here is Psalm 22:1-18 (KJV):

1My God, my God, why hast thou forsaken me? why art thou so far from helping me, and from the words of my roaring?

2O my God, I cry in the day time, but thou hearest not; and in the night season, and am not silent.

3But thou art holy, O thou that inhabitest the praises of Israel.

4Our fathers trusted in thee: they trusted, and thou didst deliver them.

5They cried unto thee, and were delivered: they trusted in thee, and were not confounded.

6But I am a worm, and no man; a reproach of men, and despised of the people.

7All they that see me laugh me to scorn: they shoot out the lip, they shake the head, saying,

8He trusted on the LORD that he would deliver him: let him deliver him, seeing he delighted in him.

9But thou art he that took me out of the womb: thou didst make me hope when I was upon my mother's breasts.

10I was cast upon thee from the womb: thou art my God from my mother's belly.

11Be not far from me; for trouble is near; for there is none to help.

12Many bulls have compassed me: strong bulls of Bashan have beset me round.

13They gaped upon me with their mouths, as a ravening and a roaring lion.

14I am poured out like water, and all my bones are out of joint: my heart is like wax; it is melted in the midst of my bowels.

15My strength is dried up like a potsherd; and my tongue cleaveth to my jaws; and thou hast brought me into the dust of death.

16For dogs have compassed me: the assembly of the wicked have inclosed me: they pierced my hands and my feet.

17I may tell all my bones: they look and stare upon me.

18They part my garments among them, and cast lots upon my vesture.

47. The Messiah would be oppressed and silent

Bible passage: Isaiah 53:7
Written: About 2,700 years ago

The 53rd chapter of the book of Isaiah contains many prophecies about a Messiah, which were fulfilled by Jesus about 700 years later. In Isaiah 53:7, the prophet spoke of the Lord's servant (the Messiah) as being oppressed and silent, like a lamb being led to its slaughter.

The words of Isaiah aptly describe what happened to Jesus about 2,000 years ago, when he was being led to his execution. Many religious leaders in Jerusalem plotted to have Jesus killed. Jesus was arrested, falsely accused, put on trial, and crucified. But, like a lamb being led to its death, Jesus did not resist.

In fact, when one of Jesus' followers drew a sword and cut off the ear of one of the men who had come to arrest him, he healed the man's ear, told his followers to stop resisting, and allowed himself to be arrested. This is described in Luke 22:47-54.

Jesus continued to be cooperative during the trial that followed his arrest. During key moments of the trial, Jesus chose to be silent rather than to resist or protest the charges against him, even though his accusers were seeking to have him executed.

One example is recorded in Matthew 27:11-14, where Jesus was taken to Pontius Pilate, who had been appointed by the Romans to help govern the land of Israel. When Pilate asked Jesus a question about who Jesus is, Jesus answered. But, when his persecutors made accusations against him, Jesus was silent.

Even when Pilate asked Jesus if he had heard the accusations, Jesus continued to remain silent:

> Then said Pilate unto him, Hearest thou not how many things they witness against thee? And he answered him to never a word; insomuch that the governor marvelled greatly. (Matthew 27:13,14, KJV)

After the trial, Jesus continued to be cooperative while he was being led to Golgotha (Calvary) and while he was being crucified.

Here is Isaiah 53:7 (KJV):

He was oppressed, and he was afflicted, yet he opened not his mouth: he is brought as a lamb to the slaughter, and as a sheep before her shearers is dumb, so he openeth not his mouth.

Note: the word *dumb* in this context means *silent.*

48. The Messiah would be beaten and spat upon

Bible passage: Isaiah 50:6,7
Written: About 2,700 years ago

In the book of Isaiah, Isaiah prophetically spoke of the Lord's servant (the Messiah) as being someone who would willingly suffer. One example can be found in Isaiah 50:6,7, which says that the servant would offer his back to those who beat him, and offer his face to those who spit on him.

These things later were recorded in the New Testament as having happened to Jesus, as being among the events that occurred after his arrest and before he was crucified.

In Matthew 26:57-68, for example, the people who had arrested Jesus took him to Caiaphas, who was the high priest, and the Sanhedrin. Caiaphas asked Jesus a question: "I adjure thee by the living God, that thou tell us whether thou be the Christ, the Son of God." In response to Jesus' reply, Jesus was accused of blasphemy. Then he was spat upon, beaten, and mocked:

> Then did they spit in his face, and buffeted him; and others smote him with the palms of their hands, Saying, Prophesy unto us, thou Christ, Who is he that smote thee? (Matthew 26:67,68, KJV)

And, in Matthew 27:11–26, Jesus was flogged after being questioned by the governor, Pontius Pilate.

- - -

Here is Isaiah 50:6,7 (KJV):

6I gave my back to the smiters, and my cheeks to them that plucked off the hair: I hid not my face from shame and spitting.

7For the Lord GOD will help me; therefore shall I not be confounded: therefore have I set my face like a flint, and I know that I shall not be ashamed.

49. The Messiah would be 'numbered with the transgressors'

Bible passage: Isaiah 53:12a
Written: About 2,700 years ago

In Isaiah 53:12, Isaiah prophesied that the Messiah would be "numbered with the transgressors," even though he was righteous (Isaiah 53:11) and had done no violence and had spoken no lies (Isaiah 53:9).

As explained in the New Testament, Jesus led a perfect and sinless life. Even so, he was falsely accused of being a criminal and he was crucified with two other men, both of whom were criminals deemed worthy of execution. In the Gospel of Mark, the author wrote the following in regards to the crucifixion of Jesus:

> And with him they crucify two thieves; the one on his right hand, and the other on his left. And the scripture was fulfilled, which saith, And he was numbered with the transgressors. (Mark 15:27,28, KJV)

- - -

Here is Isaiah 53:12a (KJV):

Therefore will I divide him a portion with the great, and he shall divide the spoil with the strong; because he hath poured out his soul unto death: and he was numbered with the transgressors; …

50. **The Messiah would intercede for sinners**

Bible passage: Isaiah 53:12b
Written: About 2,700 years ago

In the last part of Isaiah 53:12, the prophet Isaiah described the Messiah as interceding on behalf of sinners:

> and he bare the sin of many, and made intercession for the transgressors. (Isaiah 53:12b, KJV)

The New Testament of the Bible describes Jesus as having died for our sins. It also says that he intercedes for us. One example can be found in Hebrews 7:23–25. Another can be found in the book of Romans:

> He that spared not his own Son, but delivered him up for us all, how shall he not with him also freely give us

> all things? Who shall lay any thing to the charge of God's elect? It is God that justifieth. Who is he that condemneth? It is Christ that died, yea rather, that is risen again, who is even at the right hand of God, who also maketh intercession for us. (Romans 8:32-34, KJV)

In fact, even while dying on the cross, Jesus prayed for the people who had crucified him:

> Then said Jesus, Father, forgive them; for they know not what they do. (Luke 23:34a, KJV)

Chapter 6
10 other prophecies involving Jesus

Many of the Bible prophecies selected for review in this chapter involve the death, resurrection and impact of Jesus. Of all the people who have ever lived, Jesus is uniquely associated with the act of dying for the sins of others, and with the predicting of his own death and resurrection, and with having the power to resurrect others.

51. The Messiah would die

Bible passage: Isaiah 53:8,9
Written: About 2,700 years ago

In Isaiah 53:8,9, the prophet said that the Messiah would be "cut off out of the land of the living," for the sins of others.

Isaiah, who lived about seven centuries before the time of Jesus, prophesied many details about the Messiah. Here, in these verses, Isaiah prophesied that the Messiah would die, even though "he had done no violence, neither was any deceit in his mouth."

The people who wrote the books of the New Testament testify that Jesus lived a perfect and sinless life (Hebrews 4:14-16, etc). Even so, Jesus was falsely accused, put on trial and executed, about 2,000 years ago. His crucifixion and death are described in Matthew 27, Mark 15, Luke 23, and John 19.

- - -

Here is Isaiah 53:8,9 (KJV):

8He was taken from prison and from judgment: and who shall declare his generation? for he was cut off out of the land of the living: for the transgression of my people was he stricken.

9And he made his grave with the wicked, and with the rich in his death; because he had done no violence, neither was any deceit in his mouth.

52. **The Messiah would suffer for the sins of others**

Bible passage: Isaiah 53:4-6
Written: About 2,700 years ago

In Isaiah 53:4-6, the prophet, who lived about 700 years before the time of Jesus, spoke of the Messiah as suffering for the sins of others:

> Surely he hath borne our griefs, and carried our sorrows: yet we did esteem him stricken, smitten of God, and afflicted. But he was wounded for our transgressions, he was bruised for our iniquities: the chastisement of our peace was upon him; and with his stripes we are healed. All we like sheep have gone astray; we have turned every one to his own way; and the LORD hath laid on him the iniquity of us all. (Isaiah 53:4-6, KJV)

Christians believe that Jesus is the fulfillment of this prophecy, that he suffered and died for our sins, that he paid the price for all of our sins. Sin and atonement are themes that run throughout the span of the Bible, from the book of Genesis, which is the first book in the Bible, to the book of Revelation, which is the last book in the Bible. Sin separates people from God. This is expressed throughout the Bible, including in the following verses:

> But your iniquities have separated between you and your God, and your sins have hid his face from you, that he will not hear. (Isaiah 59:2, KJV)

> For all have sinned, and come short of the glory of God; (Romans 3:23, KJV)

> For the wages of sin is death; but the gift of God is eternal life through Jesus Christ our Lord. (Romans 6:23, KJV)

But, Jesus paid the price of sin. He did this by suffering and dying, in our place, as the substitute for all sinners, when he was crucified about 2,000 years ago. He died for us, and through him we have life - the gift of eternal life with God. These things are expressed in various places, including in the following verses:

> Just as man is destined to die once, and after that to face judgment, so Christ was sacrificed once to take away the sins of many people; and he will appear a second time, not to bear sin, but to bring salvation to those who are waiting for him. (Hebrews 9:27,28, NIV)

> For God so loved the world that he gave his one and only Son, that whoever believes in him shall not perish but have eternal life. (John 3:16, NIV)

> He is the atoning sacrifice for our sins, and not only for ours but also for the sins of the whole world. (1 John 2:2, NIV)

Incidentally, it is interesting to note that for centuries the Jews used the Temple in Jerusalem for a yearly ceremony, involving sacrifice, in which an offering was made for sin atonement. The ceremony was part of a day called Yom Kippur, or Day of Atonement. But, during the century in which Jesus became the permanent and once-and-for-all atonement for sin, the Temple was destroyed by the Romans, in 70 AD. And the Temple has never been rebuilt.

There is additional information in the Talmud about Yom Kippur that might prove of interest. The Talmud was compiled in written form from about 200 AD to about 500 AD. It includes Rabbinical discussions and commentary, often focusing on Judaic law, customs and ceremonies. In the Talmud, there is a passage that says that the Day of Atonement ceremony failed to work properly about 40 years before the Temple was destroyed. Among other things, according to the Talmud, there was a red piece of cloth that was supposed to turn white:

> The rabbis taught: Forty years before the Temple was destroyed, the lot never came into the right hand, the red wool did not become white, the western light did not burn, and the gates of the Temple opened of themselves, till the time that R. Johanan b. Zakkai rebuked them, saying: 'Temple, Temple, why alarmest thou us? We know that thou art destined to be destroyed.'
> - *Babylonian Talmud,* Tract Yomah, Chapter IV, as translated by Michael L. Rodkinson.

In other words, according to the Talmud, Judaism's yearly atonement ceremony stopped working properly in or around the year 30 AD. That would correspond to either the same year, or about the same year, that Jesus became the permanent atonement for sin.

53. **Zechariah foreshadowed the death of Jesus**

Bible passage: Zechariah 12:10
Written: About 2,500 years ago

In Zechariah 12:10, Zechariah was given a prophecy in which God spoke of people mourning for one who was pierced, as one would mourn over the death of an only son:

> And I will pour upon the house of David, and upon the inhabitants of Jerusalem, the spirit of grace and of supplications: and they shall look upon me whom they have pierced, and they shall mourn for him, as one mourneth for his only son, and shall be in bitterness for him, as one that is in bitterness for his firstborn. (Zechariah 12:10, KJV)

This verse, which was written about 500 years before the time of Jesus, is referred to in the Gospel of John in connection with the death of Jesus:

> The Jews therefore, because it was the preparation, that the bodies should not remain upon the cross on the sabbath day, (for that sabbath day was an high day,) besought Pilate that their legs might be broken, and that they might be taken away. Then came the soldiers, and brake the legs of the first, and of the other which was crucified with him. But when they came to Jesus, and saw that he was dead already, they brake not his legs: But one of the soldiers with a spear pierced his side, and forthwith came there out blood and water. And he that saw it bare record, and his record is true: and he knoweth that he saith true, that ye might believe. For these things were done, that the scripture should be fulfilled, A bone of him shall not be broken.

> And again another scripture saith, They shall look on him whom they pierced. (John 19:31-37, KJV)

Jesus, who is the only begotten son of God (John 3:16), was pierced while he was being crucified, when his hands and feet were nailed to the cross. And, before Jesus had been taken down from the cross, he was pierced again, with a spear by a Roman soldier.

54. **Jesus foretold his death and resurrection**

Bible passage: Matthew 20:17-19
Written: During the first century AD, about 2,000 years ago

One of the unique qualities about Jesus Christ as a religious figure is that he prophesied his own death and resurrection.

Some examples of this can be found in the Gospel of Matthew, in Matthew 16:21; 17:22,23; and 20:17-19. Jesus prophesied to his Apostles that he would be condemned, handed over to the Gentiles, mocked, flogged, and crucified, and that he would rise from the dead:

> And Jesus going up to Jerusalem took the twelve disciples apart in the way, and said unto them, Behold, we go up to Jerusalem; and the Son of man shall be betrayed unto the chief priests and unto the scribes, and they shall condemn him to death, And shall deliver him to the Gentiles to mock, and to scourge, and to crucify him: and the third day he shall rise again. (Matthew 20:17-19, KJV)

Jesus told his followers that he would die and be resurrected. Had he failed to be resurrected, his followers, obviously, would have had reason to conclude that he was a false prophet. And it would have been difficult, perhaps impossible, for Christianity to have continued as a movement in which its adherents evangelized about Jesus, and his resurrection, even at the risk of losing their own lives.

Each of the four Gospels describe the resurrection of Jesus: Matthew 28, Mark 16, Luke 24, and John 20. And the resurrection is noted in other portions of the New Testament, including an example found in Acts 9. There, a man named Paul, who had been persecuting Christians, encountered Jesus years after the resurrection. Paul converted to Christianity, became an evangelist, and traveled thousands of miles by land and by sea to tell people about Jesus.

55. **The book of Job foreshadows details of resurrection**

Bible passage: Job 19:25-27
Written: Before the time of Jesus

Christians believe in resurrection. Christians believe that people who have died will be resurrected when Jesus returns to judge the living and the dead. Their bodies will be restored to life and their souls will be reunited with their bodies.

The Old Testament of the Bible contains prophecies about resurrection. Some examples can be found in Daniel 12:1,2; Psalm 16:10; and in the book of Job:

> I know that my Redeemer lives, and that in the end he will stand upon the earth. And after my skin has been destroyed, yet in my flesh I will see God; I myself will see him with my own eyes—I, and not another. How my heart yearns within me! (Job 19:25-27, NIV)

56. **King David prophesied about resurrection**

Bible passage: Psalm 16:8-11
Written: As early as about 1000 BC, about 3,000 years ago

In Psalm 16, King David prophesied about the resurrection of Jesus:

> I have set the LORD always before me: because he is at my right hand, I shall not be moved. Therefore my heart is glad, and my glory rejoiceth: my flesh also shall rest in hope. For thou wilt not leave my soul in hell; neither wilt thou suffer thine Holy One to see corruption. Thou wilt shew me the path of life: in thy presence is fulness of joy; at thy right hand there are pleasures for evermore. (Psalm 16:8-11, KJV)

The word *corruption* in verse 10 refers to the decay of a body after death. Resurrection involves restoring a body to life and reuniting it with its soul.

Peter, who was one of the Apostles, said in the New Testament book of Acts, chapter 2, that David was speaking prophetically about the resurrection of Jesus:

> He seeing this before spake of the resurrection of Christ, that his soul was not left in hell, neither his flesh did see corruption. This Jesus hath God raised up, whereof we all are witnesses. (Acts 2:31-32, KJV)

When Jesus was about to die on the cross, about 2,000 years ago, he committed his spirit into the hands of God the Father (Luke 23:46). His body was later placed in a tomb. But, God did not abandon him to the grave. Jesus rose from the dead on the third day.

57. **Jesus announced that he is the resurrection**

Bible passage: John 11:23-27
Written: During the first century AD, about 2,000 years ago

In John 11, Jesus announced that he is "the resurrection, and the life."

In this chapter in the book of John, Jesus is recorded as comforting a woman named Martha. Her brother, Lazarus, had died days earlier. Jesus told her that her brother would rise again:

> Jesus saith unto her, Thy brother shall rise again.
>
> Martha saith unto him, I know that he shall rise again in the resurrection at the last day.
>
> Jesus said unto her, I am the resurrection, and the life: he that believeth in me, though he were dead, yet shall he live: And whosoever liveth and believeth in me shall never die. Believest thou this?
>
> She saith unto him, Yea, Lord: I believe that thou art the Christ, the Son of God, which should come into the world. (John 11:23-27, KJV)

In verse 25, Jesus informs us that he is the resurrection and that believers who die will be resurrected to eternal life with God.

58. **King David's throne would be established forever**

Bible passage: 2 Samuel 7:16

Written: Samuel lived about 3,000 years ago

In 2 Samuel 7:16, we are told that the throne of David would be established forever.

King David lived about 3,000 years ago. He was the second king of Israel, and it was his descendants, rather than those of the first king, Saul, who reigned on the throne in Jerusalem for nearly four centuries after David's death.

The succession of reigning Davidic kings came to a temporary end after the Babylonians had conquered Jerusalem and the surrounding area, about 2,600 years ago.

Then, about 2,000 years ago, Jesus became the final person recorded in the Bible as being a king of Davidic descent. Jesus is recorded in Matthew 1:1-17 as being a descendant of King David through Jesus' adoptive father, Joseph. And, in Luke 3:23-38, Jesus also is recorded as being a descendant of King David. Some scholars believe that the genealogy provided by Luke traces Jesus' ancestry through his mother, Mary.

Jesus Christ is true God and true man. He is fully divine and fully human at the same time. As such, he is a descendant of King David and he is uniquely able to preside over an everlasting kingdom.

\- - -

Here is 2 Samuel 7:16 (KJV):

And thine house and thy kingdom shall be established for ever before thee: thy throne shall be established for ever.

59. **Another prophetic promise about**

the permanence of David's throne

Bible passage: Psalm 89:34-37
Written: As early as about 3,000 years ago

In Psalm 89, there is another promise from God involving the permanence of David's throne. In reference to David, God said, "His seed shall endure for ever, and his throne as the sun before me" (Psalm 89:36, KJV).

This is fulfilled by Jesus. As a human, he is a descendant of David. And because Jesus is also fully God, he is uniquely able to reign forever as King.

- - -

Here is Psalm 89:34-37 (KJV):

34My covenant will I not break, nor alter the thing that is gone out of my lips.

35Once have I sworn by my holiness that I will not lie unto David.

36His seed shall endure for ever, and his throne as the sun before me.

37It shall be established for ever as the moon, and as a faithful witness in heaven. Selah.

60. God's salvation would reach the ends of the earth

Bible passage: Isaiah 49:6
Written: About 2,700 years ago

In Isaiah 49:6, Isaiah prophesied of a servant of God (the

Messiah) who would bring God's salvation to people throughout the world.

Jesus, as history shows, is the first and only person to be widely accepted as being the Messiah who was promised by Isaiah and other prophets of the Old Testament. And, the message of Jesus, including God's offer of salvation through Jesus (John 3:16; Romans 10:9,10; Acts 4:10-12; etc.), has been evangelized to people throughout the world.

In Acts 13:47, Paul quoted from Isaiah 49:6 in reference to evangelizing to Gentiles.

- - -

Here is Isaiah 49:6 (KJV):

And he said, It is a light thing that thou shouldest be my servant to raise up the tribes of Jacob, and to restore the preserved of Israel: I will also give thee for a light to the Gentiles, that thou mayest be my salvation unto the end of the earth.

Chapter 7
10 prophecies given by Jesus Christ

This chapter offers commentary on a selection of prophecies that Jesus gave during his public ministry, about 2,000 years ago.

61. Jesus prophesied that the Temple would be destroyed

Bible passage: Matthew 24:1,2
Written: During the first century AD, about 2,000 years ago

In Matthew 24:1,2, Jesus prophesied that the Temple in Jerusalem would be destroyed and that its destruction would be so complete that not one stone would be left standing on top of another. This prophecy was fulfilled about 40 years later.

During a war between the Jews and the Romans that ended in 70 AD, the Temple was set on fire and was torn down. The event was recorded by a Jewish historian named Josephus. He wrote that the Temple's demolition was so complete that even the foundation was destroyed:

> And I cannot but wish that we had all died before we had seen that holy city demolished by the hands of our enemies, or the foundations of our holy temple dug up after so profane a manner.
> - Josephus, *The Wars of the Jews,* Book VII, Chapter 8.

Prior to the time of Jesus, the Temple had a long history. The first Temple was built during the time of King Solomon, about 3,000 years ago. It was destroyed by the Babylonians about 2,600 years ago. The Jews later rebuilt the Temple, as a modest structure. Centuries later, King Herod commissioned a project to upgrade the Temple into a magnificent structure.

If we accept commonly assigned dates for milestones involving the Temple's history, the first Temple was destroyed in 586 BC and was rebuilt and re-consecrated about 70 years later. The second Temple stood for about 586 years and was destroyed in 70 AD.

Since the time of the destruction that Jesus had foretold, the Temple has never been rebuilt. In fact, its destruction more than 1,900 years ago was so complete, as Jesus had indicated in Matthew 24:1,2, that its exact location is still debated today.

- - -

Here is Matthew 24:1,2 (KJV):

1And Jesus went out, and departed from the temple: and his disciples came to him for to shew him the buildings of the temple.

2And Jesus said unto them, See ye not all these things? verily I say unto you, There shall not be left here one stone upon another, that shall not be thrown down.

62. **Jesus prophesied that the Jews would be exiled**

Bible passage: Luke 21:24

Written: During the first century AD, about 2,000 years ago

In Luke 21:24, Jesus prophesied that the Jews would be exiled from their land. This prophecy was fulfilled, beginning about 40 years later.

The Jews fought two wars against the Romans in the hopes of reclaiming independence for their homeland. The first war ended in 70 AD and the second war ended in 135 AD. In both wars, the Jews were defeated and forced into exile.

Josephus, the Jewish historian who witnessed the fall of Jerusalem during the first century, claimed that nearly 100,000 people were forced into exile:

> Now the number of those that were carried captive during this whole war was collected to be ninety-seven thousand;
> - Josephus, *The Wars of the Jews,* Book VI, Chapter 9.

The conquest during the second century culminated with another exile, as well as a decree prohibiting the exiled Jews from returning to Jerusalem:

> When the siege had lasted a long time, and the rebels had been driven to the last extremity by hunger and thirst, and the instigator of the rebellion had suffered his just punishment, the whole nation was prohibited from this time on by a decree, and by the commands of Adrian, from ever going up to the country about Jerusalem. For the emperor gave orders that they should not even see from a distance the land of their fathers. Such is the account of Aristo of Pella. And thus, when the city had been emptied of the Jewish nation and had suffered the total destruction of its ancient inhabitants, it was colonized by a different

> race, and the Roman city which subsequently arose changed its name and was called AElia, in honor of the emperor AElius Adrian.
> - *The Church History of Eusebius,* Book IV, Chapter 6.

The extent to which the decree was enforced is unclear. Some Jews later returned from exile. Today, according to some estimates involving the world's Jewish population, about one-third are residing within the modern state of Israel and about two-thirds are residing in communities all over the world.

- - -

Here is Luke 21:24 (KJV):

And they shall fall by the edge of the sword, and shall be led away captive into all nations: and Jerusalem shall be trodden down of the Gentiles, until the times of the Gentiles be fulfilled.

63. Jesus explained why Jerusalem would be destroyed

Bible passage: Luke 19:41-44
Written: During the first century AD, about 2,000 years ago

In Luke 19:41-44, Jesus prophesied that Jerusalem would be destroyed because the people "did not recognize the time of God's coming to you."

Although some people accepted Jesus as the Messiah, many rejected him. The rejection was strong enough that Jesus was crucified a short time later.

The destruction of Jerusalem followed about 40 years after the crucifixion, when the Romans suppressed a Jewish uprising for independence.

The Romans surrounded the city, cutting off its food supply and forcing the people within the city into starvation. These events were described by Josephus, a Jewish historian who lived during the first century, in *The Wars of the Jews,* Book V, Chapters 11 and 12.

That war lasted about 3.5 years, ending in 70 AD, with a Roman victory and a total destruction of Jerusalem and the Temple. According to Josephus, 1.1 million Jews died during the war and thousands of others were forced into exile.

During the second century of this era, when the Jews staged another uprising against the Romans, Jerusalem again was destroyed.

Cassius Dio, a Roman historian who lived during the second and third centuries, claimed that the destruction of the Jewish homeland was complete enough to embolden wild animals that otherwise would shy away from human settlements:

> Thus nearly the whole of Judaea was made desolate, an event of which the people had had indications even before the war. The tomb of Solomon, which these men regarded as one of their sacred objects, fell to pieces of itself and collapsed and many wolves and hyenas rushed howling into their cities.
> - *Roman History,* Book 69, as translated by Herbert Baldwin Foster.

- - -

Here is Luke 19:41-44 (NIV):

41 As he approached Jerusalem and saw the city, he wept
over it

42 and said, "If you, even you, had only known on this day
what would bring you peace—but now it is hidden from
your eyes.

43 The days will come upon you when your enemies will
build an embankment against you and encircle you and
hem you in on every side.

44 They will dash you to the ground, you and the children
within your walls. They will not leave one stone on
another, because you did not recognize the time of God's
coming to you."

64. Jesus forewarned that his followers would be persecuted

Bible passage: John 15:20
Written: During the first century AD, about 2,000 years ago

Among the prophecies that Jesus gave to his followers was one in which he forewarned that they, like him, would face persecution. In one example, Jesus said:

> Remember the word that I said unto you, The servant is not greater than his lord. If they have persecuted me, they will also persecute you; . . . (John 15:20, KJV)

The Bible records several persecutions of Christians. Here are some examples from the book of Acts, which is a part of the Bible that describes events after the resurrection of Jesus:

• The Apostles Peter and John were jailed after preaching about the resurrection of Jesus (Acts 4:1-4).

• The Apostles were arrested and jailed after performing miracles in which people were healed of various ailments (Acts 5:12-18).

• Many of the Christians in Jerusalem were persecuted and scattered throughout Judea and Samaria, preaching wherever they went. (Acts 8:1-4).

• King Herod (King Herod Agrippa I, grandson of Herod the Great) persecuted Christians. He arrested Peter and executed James the Apostle. (Acts 12:1–4).

• Paul and Silas were jailed in Philippi (Acts 16:16-40). Paul also was arrested in Jerusalem (Acts 21:27-36), imprisoned in Caesarea (Acts 23:23-26:32), and placed under house arrest for two years in Rome (Acts 28:16-31).

Outside of the Bible, there are many other examples of writings depicting the persecutions of Christians. During the first three centuries of its existence, Christianity was not a legally recognized religion within the Roman Empire, and Christians often fell prey to persecutions.

One example is expressed in the writings of Pliny the Younger, who was governor of the Roman province of Bithynia, which is now part of modern-day Turkey. He wrote letters to Roman Emperor Trajan, seeking advice on how to govern. In about the year 112 AD, he wrote the following in requesting advice on how to persecute Christians:

> It is my constant method to apply myself to you for the resolution of all my doubts ; for who can better govern my dilatory way of proceeding, or instruct my ignorance? I have never been present at the examination of the Christians [by others,] on which account I am unacquainted with what uses to be inquired into, and what, and how far, they used to be punished ; nor are my doubts small, whether there be not a distinction to be made between the ages [of the accused]? and whether tender youth ought to have the same punishment with strong men? Whether there be not room for pardon upon repentance? Or whether it may not be an advantage to one that had been a Christian, that he hath forsaken Christianity? Whether the bare name, without any crime besides, or the crimes adhering to that name, be to be punished?
>
> In the meantime, I have taken this course about those who have been brought before me as Christians. I asked them whether they were Christians or not? If they confessed that they were Christians, I asked them again, and a third time, intermixing threatenings with the questions. If they persevered in their confession, I ordered them to be executed ; for I did not doubt but, let their confession be of any sort whatsoever, this positiveness and inflexible obstinacy deserved to be punished.
> - *Pliny's Epistle to Trajan, About A.D. 112,* as translated by William Whiston.

Despite the persecutions, Christianity spread quickly throughout the Roman world, becoming the predominant religion. Christianity later became the first religion to spread to places throughout the world.

65. **Jesus forewarned his followers about being put to death**

Bible passage: John 16:2-3

Written: During the first century AD, about 2,000 years ago

In John 16, Jesus forewarned his followers that there would come a time when their persecutors would think that they were doing God's work by killing Jesus' followers:

> . . . yea, the time cometh, that whosoever killeth you will think that he doeth God service. And these things will they do unto you, because they have not known the Father, nor me. (John 16:2-3, KJV)

The Bible's book of Acts records the deaths of some of the first Christians, including Stephen (Acts 7:1-8:3) and James the Apostle (Acts 12:1–4).

And, Paul, while he was evangelizing in Lystra, was attacked by a mob to the extent that it was assumed that he was dead (Acts 14:8-20).

Before Paul became a Christian, he too participated in the persecution of Christians, some of whom were executed. Paul admitted this in Acts 26:

> I verily thought with myself, that I ought to do many things contrary to the name of Jesus of Nazareth. Which thing I also did in Jerusalem: and many of the saints did I shut up in prison, having received authority from the chief priests; and when they were put to death, I gave my voice against them. And I punished them oft in every synagogue, and compelled them to blaspheme; and being exceedingly mad against them, I persecuted them even unto strange cities. (Acts 26:9-11, KJV)
>
> Note: the word *strange* in this context means *foreign.*

Outside of the Bible, some early Christian writers also wrote that some of Jesus' disciples were persecuted to the point of death. One example can be found in the writings of Clement, who lived during the first century. Clement wrote that Peter, Paul, and other early Christian evangelists died as martyrs, due to the "envy" of their persecutors:

> Through envy and jealousy, the greatest and most righteous pillars [of the Church] have been persecuted and put to death. Let us set before our eyes the illustrious apostles. Peter, through unrighteous envy, endured not one or two, but numerous labours and when he had at length suffered martyrdom, departed to the place of glory due to him. Owing to envy, Paul also obtained the reward of patient endurance, after being seven times thrown into captivity, compelled to flee, and stoned. After preaching both in the east and west, he gained the illustrious reputation due to his faith, having taught righteousness to the whole world, and come to the extreme limit of the west, and suffered martyrdom under the prefects. Thus was he removed from the world, and went into the holy place, having proved himself a striking example of patience.
> - *The First Epistle of Clement to the Corinthians,* Chapter V.

66. **Jesus prophesied that he would be rejected**

Bible passage: Luke 20:9-19
Written: During the first century AD, about 2,000 years ago

During the course of Jesus' public ministry, the chief priests and other influential community members in Jerusalem often challenged Jesus and plotted against him.

One example can be found in Luke 20, where Jesus' authority was being questioned. Jesus then gave a parable in which he foretold that he would be rejected. In verse 19, Luke wrote that it was understood by the chief priests and scribes that the parable had been spoken against them.

Some examples of Jesus being rejected can be found in Matthew 26:57-68 and Matthew 27:11-31.

- - -

Here is Luke 20:9-19 (KJV):

9 Then began he to speak to the people this parable; A
certain man planted a vineyard, and let it forth to
husbandmen, and went into a far country for a long time.

10 And at the season he sent a servant to the husbandmen,
that they should give him of the fruit of the vineyard: but
the husbandmen beat him, and sent him away empty.

11 And again he sent another servant: and they beat him
also, and entreated him shamefully, and sent him away
empty.

12 And again he sent a third: and they wounded him also,
and cast him out.

13 Then said the lord of the vineyard, What shall I do? I will
send my beloved son: it may be they will reverence him
when they see him.

14 But when the husbandmen saw him, they reasoned
among themselves, saying, This is the heir: come, let us kill
him, that the inheritance may be ours.

15 So they cast him out of the vineyard, and killed him.
What therefore shall the lord of the vineyard do unto them?

16 He shall come and destroy these husbandmen, and shall give the vineyard to others. And when they heard it, they said, God forbid.

17 And he beheld them, and said, What is this then that is written, The stone which the builders rejected, the same is become the head of the corner?

18 Whosoever shall fall upon that stone shall be broken; but on whomsoever it shall fall, it will grind him to powder.

19 And the chief priests and the scribes the same hour sought to lay hands on him; and they feared the people: for they perceived that he had spoken this parable against them.

67. **Jesus prophesied about his death**

Bible passage: John 12:20-26
Written: During the first century AD, about 2,000 years ago

In John 12:20-26, Jesus, referring to himself as the "Son of man," prophesied that his death would have an impact:

> And Jesus answered them, saying, The hour is come, that the Son of man should be glorified. Verily, verily, I say unto you, Except a corn of wheat fall into the ground and die, it abideth alone: but if it die, it bringeth forth much fruit. (John 12:23,24, KJV)

Christianity teaches that through the death of Jesus, our sins are atoned for (1 John 2:2). And, that by believing in Jesus, we are given eternal life in heaven with God (John 3:16). After the death and resurrection of Jesus, evangelists traveled throughout the world to tell others about Jesus and the salvation that is found in him.

- - -

Here is John 12:20-26 (KJV):

20 And there were certain Greeks among them that came up to worship at the feast:

21 The same came therefore to Philip, which was of Bethsaida of Galilee, and desired him, saying, Sir, we would see Jesus.

22 Philip cometh and telleth Andrew: and again Andrew and Philip tell Jesus.

23 And Jesus answered them, saying, The hour is come, that the Son of man should be glorified.

24 Verily, verily, I say unto you, Except a corn of wheat fall into the ground and die, it abideth alone: but if it die, it bringeth forth much fruit.

25 He that loveth his life shall lose it; and he that hateth his life in this world shall keep it unto life eternal.

26 If any man serve me, let him follow me; and where I am, there shall also my servant be: if any man serve me, him will my Father honour.

68. Jesus prophesied that he would be resurrected in three days

Bible passage: John 2:18-22
Written: During the first century AD, about 2,000 years

ago

As mentioned elsewhere in this book, the Apostles of Jesus were able to see whether the prophecies that Jesus gave about himself were fulfilled. John recorded an example of this in John 2:18-22.

In those verses, Jesus gave a prophecy foretelling his death and resurrection. Later, after Jesus had been executed, the Apostles were able to see that Jesus had been resurrected, three days after the crucifixion. John noted this in verse 22.

- - -

Here is John 2:18-22 (KJV):

18 Then answered the Jews and said unto him, What sign shewest thou unto us, seeing that thou doest these things?

19 Jesus answered and said unto them, Destroy this temple, and in three days I will raise it up.

20 Then said the Jews, Forty and six years was this temple in building, and wilt thou rear it up in three days?

21 But he spake of the temple of his body.

22 When therefore he was risen from the dead, his disciples remembered that he had said this unto them; and they believed the scripture, and the word which Jesus had said.

69. **Jesus prophesied that the Gospel will be preached worldwide**

Bible passage: Matthew 24:14
Written: During the first century AD, about 2,000 years

ago

In Matthew 24, Jesus promised that the Gospel would be preached to people throughout the world:

> And this gospel of the kingdom shall be preached in all the world for a witness unto all nations; and then shall the end come. (Matthew 24:14, KJV)

The word Gospel means "good news." It refers to the good news that by the grace of God our sins are removed because of the redeeming work of Jesus Christ.

The good news of salvation in Christ, as expressed in John 3:16 and elsewhere in the Bible, has been taught to people throughout the world, and evangelists continue to teach people about the good news of salvation.

70. Jesus said his words will never pass away

Bible passage: Luke 21:33
Written: During the first century AD, about 2,000 years ago

Jesus, who had given prophecies about the demise of the Temple and about the end of the world, also prophesied that his words would never pass away:

> Heaven and earth shall pass away: but my words shall not pass away. (Luke 21:33, KJV)

Of the hundreds of millions of people who have ever lived, the words of only a small percentage are remembered beyond the generation that follows them. But, 2,000 years later, after Jesus had spoken the prophecy in Luke 21:33, the words of Jesus are everywhere, having been taught to people all over the world.

The words of Jesus are recorded in the Bible, especially in the Gospels, which are the New Testament books of Matthew, Mark, Luke, and John. The Bible, by the way, is said to be the most published book of all time. By some estimates, including one published in the book, the *Top 10 of Everything 2007,* by Russell Ash, the Bible has been printed at least 6 billion times throughout history. That would represent, at minimum, about one copy for every man, woman, and child alive today.

The Bible was one of the first books to be produced on the movable-type printing press that was invented during the 1400s by Johannes Gutenberg.

As of 2006, portions of the Bible, ranging from one part of the Bible to the whole Bible, have been translated into more than 2,400 languages, according to the *2006 Scripture Language Report,* which was published by the United Bible Societies. According to that report: "By the time UBS celebrated the bicentenary of the Bible Society movement in 2004, 95 per cent of the world's population theoretically had access to Scripture in a language they could understand, although not necessarily their first language."

Chapter 8
10 prophecies fulfilled by Nineveh and Babylon

These 10 Bible prophecies were fulfilled by the ancient cities of Babylon and Nineveh. Babylon served as the center of power for the Neo-Babylonian Empire, which destroyed Jerusalem and the Temple about 2,600 years ago. Nineveh served as the center of power for the Assyrian Empire, which devastated the northern part of Israel about 2,700 years ago.

71. Nineveh would be destroyed

Bible passage: Nahum 1:8,9
Written: Perhaps around 614 BC, about 2,600 years ago

The Old Testament book of Nahum contains many prophecies about the demise of Nineveh, which served as the capital for the Assyrian Empire. In Nahum 1:8,9, and elsewhere, the prophet said that Nineveh would come to an end.

The great city fell to a coalition of Babylonians and others about 2,600 years ago. The conquest of Nineveh contributed greatly to bringing an end to the Assyrian Empire, which included a large part of western Asia. The Assyrians controlled all or part of what is now Egypt, western Iran, Iraq, Israel, Jordan, Kuwait, Lebanon, northern Saudi Arabia, Syria, and eastern Turkey.

- - -

Here is Nahum 1:8,9 (NIV):

8but with an overwhelming flood he will make an end of Nineveh ; he will pursue his foes into darkness.

9Whatever they plot against the LORD he will bring to an end; trouble will not come a second time.

72. **Nineveh's destruction would be permanent**

Bible passage: Nahum 3:19
Written: Perhaps around 614 BC, about 2,600 years ago

In Nahum 3:19, the prophet said that Nineveh's destruction would be permanent, that Nineveh would suffer a wound from which it would never heal.

As explained by a Greek historian named Diodorus Siculus, who lived about 2,100 years ago, a coalition of Babylonians, Medes, and others, attacked the fortified city of Nineveh. The city was conquered in 612 BC, about 2,600 years ago.

By that time in history, the Assyrian Empire had already conquered the northern part of the land of Israel. In fact, the conquest led to the displacement of many people from 10 of the 12 Tribes of Israel. Those tribes are often referred to today as the "Lost Tribes of Israel."

The Assyrian Empire was known for its public displays of cruelty and harsh treatment of the peoples it conquered. At the end of verse 19, the evilness of the empire was alluded to: "for upon whom hath not thy wickedness passed continually."

Scholars are uncertain as to when exactly Nahum prophesied. Some scholars believe that he prophesied at least a few years before the conquest of Nineveh.

Some of Nahum's prophecies have long-term fulfillments that continue to be visible today, such as the prophecy that Nineveh would never recover from its defeat. It is worth noting that Babylon, one of the principal agents in the destruction of the Assyrian Empire, had been conquered earlier by the Assyrians. But, unlike Assyria, Babylon was able to recover and regain its empire.

- - -

Here is Nahum 3:19 (KJV):

There is no healing of thy bruise; thy wound is grievous: all that hear the bruit of thee shall clap the hands over thee: for upon whom hath not thy wickedness passed continually?

73. Deserters would flee from Nineveh before its conquest

Bible passage: Nahum 3:17
Written: Perhaps around 614 BC, about 2,600 years ago

As part of a broader prophecy involving Nineveh, the prophet, in Nahum 3:17, alluded to deserters fleeing from Nineveh.

Centuries later, the historian Diodorus mentioned deserters in his writings about the fall of Nineveh. In fact, he wrote that they contributed to its downfall, by supplying information to Arbaces, who helped lead the attack against Nineveh. Arbaces was able to stage a surprise attack while the king of Assyria's army was feasting and reveling:

> While his whole army was now feasting and revelling, Arbaces (receiving intelligence by some deserters of the security and intemperance of the enemy) fell in upon them suddenly in the night; and being in due order and discipline, and setting upon such as were in confusion, he being before prepared, and the other altogether unprovided, they easily broke into their camp, and made a great slaughter of some, forcing the rest into the city.
> - *The Historical Library of Diodorus the Sicilian,* Book II, Chapter 2.

Here is Nahum 3:17 (KJV):

Thy crowned are as the locusts, and thy captains as the great grasshoppers, which camp in the hedges in the cold day, but when the sun ariseth they flee away, and their place is not known where they are.

74. **Nineveh would be hit with a flood**

Bible passage: Nahum 2:6
Written: Perhaps around 614 BC, about 2,600 years ago

In Nahum 2:6, Nahum alluded to flooding as having a role in the destruction of Nineveh.

This too is consistent with details recorded in the historical writings of Diodorus. The ancient historian wrote that the soldiers who attacked Nineveh had a difficult time breaching the security walls that surrounded the city. But, a tributary or river, perhaps the Khosr or the Tigris, which Diodorus apparently mistakenly identified as the Euphrates, overflowed and aided the attacking army:

> The siege continued two years, during which time nothing was done to any purpose, save that the walls were sometimes assaulted, and the besieged penned up in the city. The third year it happened that [the] Euphrates, overflowing with continual rains, came up into a part of the city, and tore down the wall twenty furlongs in length.
> - *The Historical Library of Diodorus the Sicilian,* Book II, Chapter 2.

- - -

Here is Nahum 2:6 (KJV):

The gates of the rivers shall be opened, and the palace shall be dissolved.

75. **Nineveh would be hit with fire**

Bible passage: Nahum 3:15a
Written: Perhaps around 614 BC, about 2,600 years ago

In addition to the flooding that Nahum alluded to in Nahum 2:6, the prophet also mentioned fire in his prophecy of Nineveh's destruction. This, too, is consistent with the historical record. When archaeologists re-discovered and unearthed the lost city of Nineveh during the 1800s, they discovered a layer of ash covering the ruins.

According to the *Encyclopædia Britannica* (2008) entry for Nineveh, " ...Nineveh suffered a defeat from which it never recovered. Extensive traces of ash, representing the sack of the city by Babylonians, Scythians, and Medes in 612 bc, have been found in many parts of the Acropolis."

- - -

Here is Nahum 3:15a (KJV):

There shall the fire devour thee; the sword shall cut thee off, …

76. **The great city of Nineveh would become desolate**

Bible passage: Zephaniah 2:13
Written: About 2,600 years ago

In Zephaniah 2:13, the prophet, who lived about 2,600 years ago, prophesied that Nineveh, the great city of the Assyrian Empire, would become a dry and desolate land.

After a coalition of Babylonians and others had conquered Nineveh about 2,600 years ago, the city began declining. Eventually, the city was swallowed up by time and sand and lost for centuries.

A few centuries ago, the city was re-discovered and began a new life as an archaeological site. In speaking of Nineveh and the Assyrian Empire, Austen Henry Layard wrote the following, during the 1800s:

> It is, indeed, one of the most remarkable facts in history, that the records of an empire, so renowned for its power and civilisation, should have been entirely lost ; and that the site of a city as eminent for its splendour as its extent, should for ages have been a matter of doubt : it is not perhaps less curious that an accidental discovery should enable us to recover these records, and identify this site.
> - Layard, *Nineveh and Its Remains.*

- - -

Here is Zephaniah 2:13 (KJV):

And he will stretch out his hand against the north, and destroy Assyria; and will make Nineveh a desolation, and dry like a wilderness.

77. **Babylon would subjugate Judah for 70 years**

Bible passage: Jeremiah 25:11,12
Written: About 2,600 years ago

In Jeremiah 25:11,12, the prophet said that the Jews would suffer 70 years of Babylonian domination and that Babylon would be punished after the 70 years. Both parts of this prophecy were fulfilled.

The Babylonians, along with a coalition of others, conquered the city of Nineveh in 612 BC, which was the heart of the Assyrian Empire. The Assyrians then crowned a new king, Ashur-uballit II, and regrouped in Harran. But the Babylonians chased after them and forced the remnants of the Assyrian army to surrender. The king, perhaps put to death, was never heard from again. The Assyrian Empire had been defeated, and had lost its last king of record in 609 BC, never to recover and rise again.

With this conquest, Babylon assumed control over a vast portion of what had been the Assyrian Empire. Whereas Judah had been forced to pay tribute to Assyria, it would now be forced to serve Babylon. Babylon later asserted its dominance over Judah by taking many Jews as captives to Babylon, and by destroying Jerusalem and the Temple.

The Babylonian Empire came to an end in 539 BC, when Cyrus, a leader of Persians and Medes, conquered Babylon.

Cyrus later offered the captive Jews the freedom to return to their homeland.

Some scholars say that the 70-year period lasted from about 605 BC, which is about the time that Babylon began forcing many Jews into captivity, to about 536 BC, which is about the time that some members of the exiled community began returning to Judah.

And, there is another 70-year period that figures prominently in regards to Babylon's subjugation of Judah. The Babylonians had destroyed Jerusalem's Temple in 586 BC and the Jews rebuilt it and consecrated it in about 516 BC.

Here is Jeremiah 25:11,12 (KJV):

11And this whole land shall be a desolation, and an astonishment; and these nations shall serve the king of Babylon seventy years.

12And it shall come to pass, when seventy years are accomplished, that I will punish the king of Babylon, and that nation, saith the LORD, for their iniquity, and the land of the Chaldeans, and will make it perpetual desolations.

78. Babylon's gates would open for Cyrus

Bible passage: Isaiah 45:1
Written: About 2,700 years ago

In Isaiah 45:1, the prophet said that Cyrus would succeed in subduing the nations before him. Cyrus built a great empire, largely by bringing an end to the Babylonian Empire. Despite Babylon's remarkable defenses, which included moats, protective walls, and watchtowers, Cyrus was able to enter the city and conquer it.

The city straddled the Euphrates. The river ran under segments of the protective walls and through the city. Cyrus had an ingenious plan for gaining entry into the city. The plan, as described by Herodotus, a Greek historian who lived during the fifth century BC, involved diverting the flow of the Euphrates so that soldiers could march into the riverbed and under the protective walls.

Here is a portion of what Herodotus wrote about Cyrus and his invasion of Babylon:

> Therefore, whether it was some other man who suggested it to him when he was in a strait what to do, or whether he of himself perceived what he ought to do, he did as follows:--The main body of his army he posted at the place where the river runs into the city, and then again behind the city he set others, where the river issues forth from the city; and he proclaimed to his army that so soon as they should see that the stream had become passable, they should enter by this way into the city. Having thus set them in their places and in this manner exhorted them he marched away himself with that part of his army which was not fit for fighting: and when he came to the lake, Cyrus also did the same things which the queen of the Babylonians had done as regards the river and the lake; that is to say, he conducted the river by a channel into the lake, which was at that time a swamp, and so made the former course of the river passable by the sinking of the stream.
> - Herodotus, *The Histories,* Volume I, Book I, Section 191, as translated by G.C. Macaulay.

- - -

Here is Isaiah 45:1 (KJV):

Thus saith the LORD to his anointed, to Cyrus, whose right hand I have holden, to subdue nations before him; and I will loose the loins of kings, to open before him the two leaved gates; and the gates shall not be shut;

79. **Babylon would be overthrown**

Bible passage: Isaiah 13:19
Written: About 2,700 years ago

In Isaiah 13:19, the prophet said that Babylon would be overthrown.

About 150 years after the time of Isaiah, Cyrus, with a coalition of Medes and Persians, conquered Babylon in 539 BC, bringing an end to its empire.

After the defeat, Babylon was never able to regain its empire, even though it had accomplished a similar feat prior to the time of Cyrus. In fact, Babylon previously had been defeated by the Assyrians and was able to recover and avenge its loss by conquering the Assyrian Empire.

In the centuries following Cyrus' conquest of Babylon, the great city became desolate and forgotten.

- - -

Here is Isaiah 13:19 (KJV):

And Babylon, the glory of kingdoms, the beauty of the Chaldees' excellency, shall be as when God overthrew Sodom and Gomorrah.

80. **Babylon would be humbled**

Bible passages: Isaiah 14:23; Isaiah 13:21; Isaiah 13:19
Written: About 2,700 years ago

The book of Isaiah foretold a humble end for Babylon, despite its prior history of power and perseverance:

> I will also make it a possession for the bittern, and pools of water: and I will sweep it with the besom of destruction, saith the LORD of hosts. (Isaiah 14:23, KJV)

> But wild beasts of the desert shall lie there; and their houses shall be full of doleful creatures; and owls shall dwell there, and satyrs shall dance there. (Isaiah 13:21, KJV)

> And Babylon, the glory of kingdoms, the beauty of the Chaldees' excellency, shall be as when God overthrew Sodom and Gomorrah. (Isaiah 13:19, KJV)

Within these and other Bible verses, it was prophesied that Babylon, which had been powerful enough to dominate much of the ancient world, would be humbled to the point of desolation.

Babylon's decline began after Cyrus conquered it about 2,500 years ago. Although it had recovered marvelously from previous defeats and setbacks, Babylon never again would reclaim its past glories and power. During the centuries that followed, Babylon waned and faded and eventually fell into disrepair and desolation.

Like Nineveh, Babylon would be lost to obscurity for a time. And, like Nineveh, it would re-emerge during modern times as an archaeological site.

Archaeologists began excavating the site about 200 years ago, during the mid-1800s. Some parts of the city, however, could not be dug up because they had been overcome with water from a water table:

> The height of the water-table has tended to restrict most excavation to the Neo-Babylonian (CHALDAEAN) dynasty (c. 625-539 BC), when the political power of the Babylonians probably reached its greatest height.
> - *A Dictionary of Archaeology,* by Ian Shaw and Robert Jameson.

Chapter 9
10 prophecies fulfilled by other nations

These 10 Bible prophecies were fulfilled by ancient nations that were near the land of Israel. These nations include Edom, Tyre, and Egypt.

81. Daniel prophesied about four great kingdoms

Bible passage: Daniel 2:27-47
Written: Daniel lived more than 2,500 years ago

In Daniel 2:27-47, the prophet Daniel, who was a Jew living in Babylon as an exile, was given the power by God to interpret a dream of Nebuchadnezzar, the king of Babylon. The dream, as Daniel explained to Nebuchadnezzar, foresaw a succession of kingdoms that would rise up and become dominant world powers.

As shown in verses 32 and 33, Nebuchadnezzar's dream involved a vision of a man-like statue, which Daniel later explained in four parts, beginning with the head:

1. A head of gold.
2. A chest and arms of silver.
3. A belly and thighs of bronze.
4. And legs of iron, with feet that were part iron and part clay.

The prophetic dream described four empires, starting with

Nebuchadnezzar's Neo-Babylonian Empire, which is symbolized as the head of gold. The Neo-Babylonian Empire rose up about 2,600 years ago. The Babylonians defeated the Assyrian army in 612 BC, chased down the last Assyrian king in 609 BC, and controlled a vast empire until 539 BC.

The next great kingdom to arise was the Medo-Persian Empire, which conquered Babylon in 539 BC. Some scholars have suggested that the symbol of the two arms of silver represents the Medes and Persians, the two principal groups that comprised the heart and power of the empire.

The third kingdom is symbolized by the statue's belly and thighs of bronze. (Some English translations, such as the KJV, use the word *brass* instead of *bronze*). Many scholars understand this to be a reference to the Greek Empire, which succeeded the Medo-Persian Empire. Some commentators have proposed that the symbol of a belly and thighs suggests that the kingdom was to start out as a united kingdom but end up as a divided kingdom. After the death of Alexander the Great, the Greek Empire initially was divided up into four parts.

The symbolism of the fourth kingdom often has been recognized as a description of the Roman Empire. Some commentators have suggested that, like the legs of iron, the Roman Empire was extremely powerful, but ultimately divided.

The *Concordia Self-Study Bible NIV* offers a succinct description of the symbolism:

> The diminishing value of the metals from gold to silver to bronze to iron represents the decreasing power and grandeur (v. 39) of the rulers of the

> successive empires, from the absolute despotism of Nebuchadnezzar to the democratic system of checks and balances that characterized the Roman senates and assemblies. The metals also symbolize a growing degree of toughness and endurance, with each successive empire lasting longer than the preceding one.
> - *Concordia Self-Study Bible NIV,* footnote for Daniel 2:32-43.

Each of the four empires covered a large swath of land, including the land of Israel, in the general area of where the continents of Asia, Africa and Europe converge. And each rose to power before the completion of the Bible. The final part of the Bible - the New Testament - was completed during the first century AD, when the Roman Empire was still in power.

And, each of the four empires had a profound impact on the history of Israel. The Babylonians destroyed Jerusalem and the Temple and forced many Jews into exile. The forced exile ended by decree during the time of the Medo-Persian Empire, and the Jews were given permission to resettle and rebuild Jerusalem. The Jews later gained sovereignty for part of their homeland, during the time of the Greek Empire. And the Romans destroyed Jerusalem and the Temple and forced the Jewish people into an exile that later contributed to a worldwide dispersion.

Daniel also noted that a fifth kingdom would arise, one that would not be created by human hands, and which would not be destroyed (Daniel 2:44,45).

According to the *Concordia Self-Study Bible NIV:*

> The fifth kingdom is the eternal kingdom of God, different from the sinful and transient empires of man.

Its authority will extend over "the whole earth" (v. 35) and ultimately over "a new heaven and a new earth" (Rev. 21:1).
- *Concordia Self-Study Bible NIV,* footnote for Daniel 2:44.

Here is Daniel 2:27-47 (KJV):

27Daniel answered in the presence of the king, and said,
The secret which the king hath demanded cannot the wise
men, the astrologers, the magicians, the soothsayers, shew
unto the king;

28But there is a God in heaven that revealeth secrets, and
maketh known to the king Nebuchadnezzar what shall be in
the latter days. Thy dream, and the visions of thy head upon
thy bed, are these;

29As for thee, O king, thy thoughts came into thy mind
upon thy bed, what should come to pass hereafter: and he
that revealeth secrets maketh known to thee what shall
come to pass.

30But as for me, this secret is not revealed to me for any
wisdom that I have more than any living, but for their sakes
that shall make known the interpretation to the king, and
that thou mightest know the thoughts of thy heart.

31Thou, O king, sawest, and behold a great image. This
great image, whose brightness was excellent, stood before
thee; and the form thereof was terrible.

32This image's head was of fine gold, his breast and his
arms of silver, his belly and his thighs of brass,

33His legs of iron, his feet part of iron and part of clay.

34Thou sawest till that a stone was cut out without hands,
which smote the image upon his feet that were of iron and
clay, and brake them to pieces.

35Then was the iron, the clay, the brass, the silver, and the
gold, broken to pieces together, and became like the chaff
of the summer threshingfloors; and the wind carried them
away, that no place was found for them: and the stone that
smote the image became a great mountain, and filled the
whole earth.

36This is the dream; and we will tell the interpretation
thereof before the king.

37Thou, O king, art a king of kings: for the God of heaven
hath given thee a kingdom, power, and strength, and glory.

38And wheresoever the children of men dwell, the beasts of
the field and the fowls of the heaven hath he given into
thine hand, and hath made thee ruler over them all. Thou
art this head of gold.

39And after thee shall arise another kingdom inferior to
thee, and another third kingdom of brass, which shall bear
rule over all the earth.

40And the fourth kingdom shall be strong as iron:
forasmuch as iron breaketh in pieces and subdueth all
things: and as iron that breaketh all these, shall it break in
pieces and bruise.

41And whereas thou sawest the feet and toes, part of potters'
clay, and part of iron, the kingdom shall be divided; but

there shall be in it of the strength of the iron, forasmuch as
thou sawest the iron mixed with miry clay.

42And as the toes of the feet were part of iron, and part of
clay, so the kingdom shall be partly strong, and partly
broken.

43And whereas thou sawest iron mixed with miry clay, they
shall mingle themselves with the seed of men: but they
shall not cleave one to another, even as iron is not mixed
with clay.

44And in the days of these kings shall the God of heaven set
up a kingdom, which shall never be destroyed: and the
kingdom shall not be left to other people, but it shall break
in pieces and consume all these kingdoms, and it shall
stand for ever.

45Forasmuch as thou sawest that the stone was cut out of
the mountain without hands, and that it brake in pieces the
iron, the brass, the clay, the silver, and the gold; the great
God hath made known to the king what shall come to pass
hereafter: and the dream is certain, and the interpretation
thereof sure.

46Then the king Nebuchadnezzar fell upon his face, and
worshipped Daniel, and commanded that they should offer
an oblation and sweet odours unto him.

47The king answered unto Daniel, and said, Of a truth it is,
that your God is a God of gods, and a Lord of kings, and a
revealer of secrets, seeing thou couldest reveal this secret.

82. **Philistia would be destroyed**

Bible passage: Jeremiah 47:1-7
Written: About 2,600 years ago

The prophets of the Old Testament had much to say about the nations that had sought to harm or destroy Israel. Some of their prophecies foretold that these nations would be destroyed.

The following example involves the Philistines, who controlled a portion of land between Judah and the Mediterranean Sea. That area included the cities of Gaza, Ashkelon, Ashdod, Ekron, and Gath. At various times in history, such as during the time of King David about 3,000 years ago, the Philistines were often involved in conflicts with Israel.

About 2,600 years ago, the prophet Jeremiah proclaimed that the Philistines would be destroyed. In Jeremiah 47:1-7, the prophet announced that the real threat against the Philistines would not come from Egypt, which was about to attack the city of Gaza, but from the north, which would be the direction from which the Babylonians would invade and subdue the region.

Biblical mentions of the Philistines, as well as mentions of them in other records, decreased substantially after the time of the Babylonian invasion. Whereas the Jews recovered from their hardships and retained their national identity, the Philistines did not.

- - -

Here is Jeremiah 47:1-7 (KJV):

1 The word of the LORD that came to Jeremiah the prophet against the Philistines, before that Pharaoh smote Gaza.

2 Thus saith the LORD; Behold, waters rise up out of the

north, and shall be an overflowing flood, and shall
overflow the land, and all that is therein; the city, and them
that dwell therein: then the men shall cry, and all the
inhabitants of the land shall howl.

3 At the noise of the stamping of the hoofs of his strong
horses, at the rushing of his chariots, and at the rumbling of
his wheels, the fathers shall not look back to their children
for feebleness of hands;

4 Because of the day that cometh to spoil all the Philistines,
and to cut off from Tyrus and Zidon every helper that
remaineth: for the LORD will spoil the Philistines, the
remnant of the country of Caphtor.

5 Baldness is come upon Gaza; Ashkelon is cut off with the
remnant of their valley: how long wilt thou cut thyself?

6 O thou sword of the LORD, how long will it be ere thou
be quiet? put up thyself into thy scabbard, rest, and be still.

7 How can it be quiet, seeing the LORD hath given it a
charge against Ashkelon, and against the sea shore? there
hath he appointed it.

83. Tyre would lose its wealth and power

Bible passage: Zechariah 9:3,4
Written: About 2,500 years ago

In Zechariah 9:3,4, the prophet said that the Phoenician city of Tyre (Tyrus) would lose its power in the sea.

During the time of Zechariah, Tyre was a Phoenician colony and a dominant maritime power within the

Mediterranean Sea. The Phoenicians were among the most culturally and economically influential people within the Mediterranean world, and they enjoyed many centuries of success.

The Bible describes a trading agreement that existed between Tyre and Israel about 3,000 years ago, during the time of King Solomon. In exchange for shipments of wheat and pressed olive oil, Tyre supplied materials and skilled laborers to help with the construction of the Temple in Jerusalem (1 Kings 5:1–12).

Tyre had trading partners far beyond Israel, in every direction. Ezekiel lists several in Ezekiel 27:12-24, including places in and around present-day Armenia, Iraq, Syria, Turkey, Yemen, and possibly Spain or Sardinia.

Along with its wealth and power, Phoenician Tyre was also secure. It consisted of a mainland area and an island. By some accounts, portions of a wall protecting the island exceeded 100 feet in height.

But for all of its success, and despite its security, several prophets of the Bible, including Amos, Isaiah, and Ezekiel foretold a bleak future for Tyre.

During the time of Ezekiel, about 2,600 years ago, the Babylonians attacked the mainland of Tyre. And, about 2,300 years ago, Alexander the Great conquered the island. Alexander's conquest brought an end to the Phoenician empire and was followed by the eventual demise of the Phoenician people.

The Tyre of today is no longer a sovereign city-state, and it is no longer Phoenician. In fact, the island itself is no longer an island. It is joined to the mainland of Lebanon by means of a man-made causeway, which was created when Alexander conquered the island.

- - -

Here is Zechariah 9:3,4 (KJV):

3And Tyrus did build herself a strong hold, and heaped up silver as the dust, and fine gold as the mire of the streets.

4Behold, the LORD will cast her out, and he will smite her power in the sea; and she shall be devoured with fire.

84. Amos explained why Tyre would be punished

Bible passage: Amos 1:9,10
Written: Amos lived about 2,800 years ago

In Amos, chapter 1, Amos delivered a prophecy proclaiming that God would punish nations around Israel because of their hostility and cruelty. In the case of Tyre, it was to endure destruction because it had violated a treaty of brotherhood and had delivered captives to Edom (Amos 1:9,10).

- - -

Here is Amos 1:9,10 (KJV):

9Thus saith the LORD; For three transgressions of Tyrus, and for four, I will not turn away the punishment thereof; because they delivered up the whole captivity to Edom, and remembered not the brotherly covenant:

10But I will send a fire on the wall of Tyrus, which shall devour the palaces thereof.

85. Tyre's stones, timber, and soil would end up in the sea

Bible passage: Ezekiel 26:12
Written: About 2,600 years ago

In Ezekiel 26:12, the prophet said that Tyre's stones, timber, and soil would end up in the sea.

The details provided in this verse are similar to a description of the steps that Alexander the Great took in conquering Tyre (Tyrus), more than 2,300 years ago. In order to build a land bridge from the mainland to the island, to aid in attacking the island fortress, his army tossed the rubble from the mainland area of Tyre (Palae-Tyrus) into the Mediterranean Sea.

As explained by George Rawlinson, who was an ancient history professor during the 1800s at the University of Oxford:

> Material for the construction was abundant. The great city of Palae-Tyrus was close at hand, partly in ruins, and with many of the houses deserted by their inhabitants. Its walls would furnish abundance of stone, mortar, and rubble. . . . Whole trees, torn up by the roots, and with their branches still adhering to them, had been dragged to the water's edge, and then precipitated into the strait ; a layer of stones and mud had been placed upon them, to solidify them into a mass ; on the top of this other trees had been placed, and the former process repeated.
> - Rawlinson, *History of Phoenicia,* Chapter XIV.

Some Bible scholars, including John Gill, who was an English Baptist minister who wrote during the 1700s, described this event as being the fulfillment of Ezekiel 26:12.

- - -

Here is Ezekiel 26:12 (KJV):

And they shall make a spoil of thy riches, and make a prey of thy merchandise: and they shall break down thy walls, and destroy thy pleasant houses: and they shall lay thy stones and thy timber and thy dust in the midst of the water.

86. Tyre would be attacked by many nations and destroyed

Bible passage: Ezekiel 26:1-14
Written: About 2,600 years ago

In Ezekiel 26:1-14, the prophet gave a detailed prophecy about the destruction of Tyre (Tyrus), the great maritime city that had gloated over the fall of Jerusalem.

In verses 3-5, Ezekiel prophesied that Tyre would be attacked by many nations and that its walls and towers would be torn down.

In verses 7-11, Ezekiel described how Nebuchadnezzar, the king of Babylon, would demolish the mainland of Tyre. Nebuchadnezzar began his attack during the time of Ezekiel, about 2,600 years ago.

Tyre was a powerful and commercially successful Phoenician city. It consisted of a mainland area, which was on the eastern shore of the Mediterranean Sea, and an island within the sea.

A few centuries after Nebuchadnezzar, Alexander the Great was in the process of building his own empire, which would include the island of Tyre. Some historical sources list the date of Alexander's conquest of the island, which was in 332 BC, as being the end date for the Phoenician empire, which was never revived.

In the centuries that followed, the identity of the Phoenicians as a group of people was lost. The island fell under the rule of a succession of foreign powers and was attacked again and destroyed in 1291.

A Jewish traveler during the 1100s, named Benjamin of Tudela, visited Tyre and wrote the following:

> A man can ascend the walls of New Tyre and see ancient Tyre, which the sea has now covered, lying at a stone's throw from the new city. And should one care to go forth by boat, one can see the castles, market-places, streets, and palaces in the bed of the sea. New Tyre is a busy place of commerce, to which merchants flock from all quarters.
> - Benjamin of Tudela, *The Itinerary of Benjamin of Tudela.*

Today, it is difficult to find artifacts from the Phoenician city of Tyre that existed during Ezekiel's time. According to the *Columbia Encyclopedia* entry for Tyre: "The principal ruins of the city today are those of buildings erected by the Crusaders. There are some Greco-Roman remains, but any left by the Phoenicians lie underneath the present town."

- - -

Here is Ezekiel 26:1-14 (KJV):

1 And it came to pass in the eleventh year, in the first day of
the month, that the word of the LORD came unto me,
saying,

2 Son of man, because that Tyrus hath said against
Jerusalem, Aha, she is broken that was the gates of the
people: she is turned unto me: I shall be replenished, now
she is laid waste:

3 Therefore thus saith the Lord GOD; Behold, I am against
thee, O Tyrus, and will cause many nations to come up
against thee, as the sea causeth his waves to come up.

4 And they shall destroy the walls of Tyrus, and break down
her towers: I will also scrape her dust from her, and make
her like the top of a rock.

5 It shall be a place for the spreading of nets in the midst of
the sea: for I have spoken it, saith the Lord GOD: and it
shall become a spoil to the nations.

6 And her daughters which are in the field shall be slain by
the sword; and they shall know that I am the LORD.

7 For thus saith the Lord GOD; Behold, I will bring upon
Tyrus Nebuchadrezzar king of Babylon, a king of kings,
from the north, with horses, and with chariots, and with
horsemen, and companies, and much people.

8 He shall slay with the sword thy daughters in the field:
and he shall make a fort against thee, and cast a mount
against thee, and lift up the buckler against thee.

9 And he shall set engines of war against thy walls, and

with his axes he shall break down thy towers.

10 By reason of the abundance of his horses their dust shall
cover thee: thy walls shall shake at the noise of the
horsemen, and of the wheels, and of the chariots, when he
shall enter into thy gates, as men enter into a city wherein is
made a breach.

11 With the hoofs of his horses shall he tread down all thy
streets: he shall slay thy people by the sword, and thy
strong garrisons shall go down to the ground.

12 And they shall make a spoil of thy riches, and make a
prey of thy merchandise: and they shall break down thy
walls, and destroy thy pleasant houses: and they shall lay
thy stones and thy timber and thy dust in the midst of the
water.

13 And I will cause the noise of thy songs to cease; and the
sound of thy harps shall be no more heard.

14 And I will make thee like the top of a rock: thou shalt be
a place to spread nets upon; thou shalt be built no more: for
I the LORD have spoken it, saith the Lord GOD.

87. Egypt would no longer rule over nations

Bible passage: Ezekiel 29:15b
Written: About 2,600 years ago

In Ezekiel 29:15, the prophet proclaimed that Egypt "shall no more rule over the nations."

Up until the time of Ezekiel, Egypt had been a powerful nation for many centuries, dominating many nations, including Judah, at different times.

But, Egypt's sphere of influence was deflated about 2,600 years ago, during the time of Ezekiel. In about 605 BC, the Babylonians soundly defeated the Egyptian and Assyrian armies at Carchemish, which is near the border of Turkey and Syria. In 2 Kings, we are told of the impact that the defeat had on the Egyptian pharaoh (king):

> And the king of Egypt came not again any more out of his land: for the king of Babylon had taken from the river of Egypt unto the river Euphrates all that pertained to the king of Egypt. (2 Kings 24:7, KJV)

Since the time of Ezekiel, Egypt has spent much of its history being ruled over by other nations. Egypt's last native Pharaoh was King Nectanebo II, who was defeated by the Persians in about 343 BC, which is about 2,300 years ago. Afterwards, Egypt fell to a succession of foreign powers, including the Greeks, Romans, Ottomans, and the British.

Egypt regained sovereignty in 1922, from the British.

\- - -

Here is Ezekiel 29:15b (KJV):

... for I will diminish them, that they shall no more rule over the nations.

88. The people of Israel would take vengeance on the Edomites

Bible passage: Ezekiel 25:14
Written: About 2,600 years ago

In Ezekiel 25:14, Ezekiel foretold that the people of Israel would take vengeance on Edom, a nation that had often been hostile with Israel.

During the time in which Ezekiel delivered this prophecy, his homeland had been conquered by Babylon, and many Jews, including Ezekiel, were being forced to live in exile. But, about 400 years later, the Jews regained sovereignty for part of their homeland, including the city of Jerusalem.

During that time of sovereignty, the Jews subdued Edom, which also was known as Idumea. Josephus, a Jewish historian who lived about 2,000 years ago, wrote that a Jewish leader named Judas Maccabeus fought and defeated Edom sometime around 168 BC:

> When these things were over, the nations round about the Jews were very uneasy at the revival of their power, and rose up together, and destroyed many of them, as gaining advantage over them by laying snares for them, and making secret conspiracies against them. Judas made perpetual expeditions against these men, and endeavoured to restrain them from those incursions, and to prevent the mischiefs they did to the Jews. So he fell upon the Idumeans, the posterity of Esau, at Acrabattene, and slew a great many of them, and took their spoils.
> - Josephus, *Antiquities of the Jews,* Book XII, Chapter 8.

Decades later, around 125 BC, the Jewish priest-king John Hyrcanus I also fought with and subdued the people of Edom, who were known as Edomites or Idumeans.

Hyrcanus permitted the Edomites to remain in Edom if they adopted Jewish laws and customs, which they did, according to Josephus:

> . . . that they submitted to the use of circumcision, and of the rest of the Jewish ways of living ; at which time therefore this befell them, that they were hereafter no other than Jews.
> - *Antiquities of the Jews,* Book XIII, Chapter 9.

The Edomites lost their identity as a distinct group of people sometime around the fall of Jerusalem in 70 AD, according to the *Jewish Encyclopedia:* "From this time the Idumeans ceased to be a separate people, though the name 'Idumea' still existed [during] the time of Jerome." (Jerome was a Christian writer who lived during the fourth and fifth centuries of this era, about 1,500 years ago).

- - -

Here is Ezekiel 25:14 (KJV):

And I will lay my vengeance upon Edom by the hand of my people Israel: and they shall do in Edom according to mine anger and according to my fury; and they shall know my vengeance, saith the Lord GOD.

89. **Edom would become desolate**

Bible passage: Ezekiel 35:1-5
Written: About 2,600 years ago

In Ezekiel 35:1-5, Ezekiel prophesied that the country of Edom (mount Seir) would become desolate, because of its perpetual hatred of the people of Israel.

In the centuries that followed the time of Ezekiel, the land and people of Edom were conquered and re-conquered. The people eventually lost their identity as a separate ethnic group. And the land became isolated, forgotten, and desolate, as alluded to by various writers throughout history.

In the book, *The Biblical World,* a writer named George L. Robinson offered details as to how isolated the land of Edom was during the 1800s:

> The regions east and south of the Dead Sea have been the last portions of Palestine to be explored. ... Travel in these parts has hitherto been difficult and unsafe, owing on the one hand to the opposition of the Turkish government, which does not favor foreigners' running so great a risk, and on the other to the wild Bedouin themselves, who usually plunder those who undertake to make the expedition. Accordingly Moab, especially Edom and the northeastern portion of the peninsula of Sinai, still awaits careful exploration . . .
>
> It had been the writer's earnest wish for several years to visit Petra, the ancient capital of Edom. On arriving in Cairo, however, he sought in vain for a dragoman who was willing to venture thither from the south. In Jerusalem also no native guide had the courage necessary to make the attempt. At length an Englishman was recommended, who, having been seven years a missionary in Kerak, Moab, consented to do so, on condition that tents, equipment, and all luxury of every sort should be left behind.
> - Robinson, *The Biblical World.*

Another traveler wrote the following, which was published in 1866:

> On leaving El Uebe, (the water, by the bye, stank, and was full of worms,)--we entered the low barren ridges that skirt Wady Araba on the west, and, for several hours during this and the following day, traversed a country of the most utter desolation, hills succeeding hills, without the slightest picturesque beauty, covered with loose flints, sand, gravel ; sterility in its most

> repulsive garb ;--it made the very heart ache, and the spirits sink--and such is Edom now, "most desolate," as prophecy foretold it should be, . . .
> - *Letters on Egypt, Edom, and the Holy Land.*

Here is Ezekiel 35:1-5 (KJV):

1 Moreover the word of the LORD came unto me, saying,

2 Son of man, set thy face against mount Seir, and prophesy against it,

3 And say unto it, Thus saith the Lord GOD; Behold, O mount Seir, I am against thee, and I will stretch out mine hand against thee, and I will make thee most desolate.

4 I will lay thy cities waste, and thou shalt be desolate, and thou shalt know that I am the LORD.

5 Because thou hast had a perpetual hatred, and hast shed the blood of the children of Israel by the force of the sword in the time of their calamity, in the time that their iniquity had an end:

90. **The fate of Edom, in contrast to Israel**

Bible passage: Obadiah 1:10
Written: More than 2,000 years ago

In Genesis, we are told about twin brothers named Esau and Jacob, who were born about 4,000 years ago. Both became the patriarchs of a nation. Jacob's descendants became known as the Israelites. Esau's descendants were called Edomites or Idumeans.

Although they entered history at the same time, the Bible prophets foretold that their futures would be very different.

Edom, as many Bible prophets proclaimed, would be destroyed. One example came from the prophet Obadiah:

> For thy violence against thy brother Jacob shame shall cover thee, and thou shalt be cut off for ever. (Obadiah 1:10, KJV)

The word "Jacob" is used in this verse to refer to the people of Israel, who are the descendants of Jacob.

Edom had been a frequent enemy of Israel. In Numbers 20:14–21, when the descendants of Jacob returned from Egypt, the descendants of Esau refused to let them travel through Edom to return to the land of Israel. In fact, the Edomites threatened to attack the Israelites if they tried to pass through Edom.

Another example of conflict can be found in 1 Samuel 14:47, where Edom is listed as an enemy to Israel during the time of King Saul, about 3,000 years ago.

And, in Obadiah 1:12-14, the prophet described how the Edomites gloated during a time of calamity for the people of Judah and how the Edomites persecuted refugees as they tried to flee from Jerusalem.

But in the centuries that followed, it was Edom that the world would forget and it was Israel through which the world would be changed.

The Bible offers many statements and prophecies about the role and perseverance of the people of Israel. They were chosen to record the words of God. They were chosen to be the people from whom the Messiah would come. And Israel was chosen to be the place from which the message of salvation would extend to the ends of the earth (Isaiah 49:6; Matthew 24:14; and Acts 1:6-11).

And, indeed, as history has shown, it is from the people of Israel that the world has its most widely published book (the Bible), and its most widespread religion (Christianity), and its most widely known person (Jesus).

Chapter 10
10 End Times prophecies

These 10 Bible prophecies are related to the return of Jesus, when he is to judge the living and the dead.

91. Jesus will return in the future

Bible passage: Matthew 24:30
Written: During the first century AD, about 2,000 years ago

In Matthew 24, Jesus announced that he will return in the future. In speaking of himself, he said:

> And then shall appear the sign of the Son of man in heaven: and then shall all the tribes of the earth mourn, and they shall see the Son of man coming in the clouds of heaven with power and great glory. (Matthew 24:30, KJV)

92. Jesus will return and judge the living and the dead

Bible passage: 2 Timothy 4:1,2
Written: During the first century AD, about 2,000 years ago

In 2 Timothy 4:1,2, as well as in other verses, we are told that Jesus will judge the living and the dead, when he returns:

> In the presence of God and of Christ Jesus, who will judge the living and the dead, and in view of his appearing and his kingdom, I give you this charge: Preach the Word; be prepared in season and out of season; correct, rebuke and encourage—with great patience and careful instruction. (2 Timothy 4:1,2, NIV)

93. **When Jesus will return**

Bible passage: Matthew 24:36
Written: During the first century AD, about 2,000 years ago

Many people throughout history have falsely claimed to know when Jesus would return, only to be proven wrong, time and time again.

Jesus, however, did not provide a specific time as to when he is to return. Here are a few examples of what Jesus said in regards to his second coming:

> But of that day and hour knoweth no man, no, not the angels of heaven, but my Father only. (Matthew 24:36, KJV)

> Watch therefore: for ye know not what hour your Lord doth come. (Matthew 24:42, KJV)

The Apostle Peter also addressed the timing of the return of Jesus:

> But, beloved, be not ignorant of this one thing, that one day is with the Lord as a thousand years, and a thousand years as one day. The Lord is not slack concerning his promise, as some men count slackness; but is longsuffering to us-ward, not willing that any

> should perish, but that all should come to repentance. (2 Peter 3:8,9, KJV)

94. People will have contempt for God during the last days

Bible passage: 2 Timothy 3:1-5
Written: During the first century AD, about 2,000 years ago

In 2 Timothy, chapter 3, Paul prophesied about how people will behave during the last days. He said that they will, among other things, have love for pleasure and contempt for God.

Here is a sample from 2 Timothy 3:

> This know also, that in the last days perilous times shall come. For men shall be lovers of their own selves, covetous, boasters, proud, blasphemers, disobedient to parents, unthankful, unholy, Without natural affection, trucebreakers, false accusers, incontinent, fierce, despisers of those that are good, Traitors, heady, highminded, lovers of pleasures more than lovers of God; Having a form of godliness, but denying the power thereof: from such turn away. (2 Timothy 3:1-5, KJV)

95. There will be false prophets and false christs

Bible passages: Matthew 24:4,5; Matthew 24:11; Matthew 24:23,24
Written: During the first century AD, about 2,000 years ago

In Matthew 24, Jesus prophesied that, before he returns, there would be people falsely claiming to be prophets and falsely claiming to be Christ:

> And many false prophets shall rise, and shall deceive many. (Matthew 24:11, KJV)

> Then if any man shall say unto you, Lo, here is Christ, or there; believe it not. For there shall arise false Christs, and false prophets, and shall shew great signs and wonders; insomuch that, if it were possible, they shall deceive the very elect. (Matthew 24:23,24, KJV)

> And Jesus answered and said unto them, Take heed that no man deceive you. For many shall come in my name, saying, I am Christ; and shall deceive many. (Matthew 24:4,5, KJV)

96. **The return of Jesus will be visible and obvious to everyone**

Bible passages: Matthew 24:26,27; Revelation 1:7
Written: During the first century AD, about 2,000 years ago

In Matthew 24, Jesus forewarned that there would be false prophets and false claims involving his return. In this same chapter, Jesus also made it clear that, when he returns, his return will be obvious to everyone:

> Wherefore if they shall say unto you, Behold, he is in the desert; go not forth: behold, he is in the secret chambers; believe it not. For as the lightning cometh out of the east, and shineth even unto the west; so shall also the coming of the Son of man be. (Matthew 24:26,27, KJV)

And, we are reminded of this in the book of Revelation:

> Behold, he cometh with clouds; and every eye shall see him, and they also which pierced him: and all kindreds of the earth shall wail because of him. Even so, Amen. (Revelation 1:7, KJV)

97. The heavens and earth will be destroyed

Bible passage: 2 Peter 3:10
Written: During the first century AD, about 2,000 years ago

In 2 Peter, which is called an "epistle" or "letter," and is part of the New Testament, we again are told that the "day of the Lord" will come as a surprise, and we are told that the heavens and earth will be destroyed:

> But the day of the Lord will come as a thief in the night; in the which the heavens shall pass away with a great noise, and the elements shall melt with fervent heat, the earth also and the works that are therein shall be burned up. (2 Peter 3:10, KJV)

The epistle also says that a new heavens and earth will be created.

98. Christians should not fear the end of the world

Bible passage: 2 Peter 3:11-13
Written: During the first century AD, about 2,000 years ago

In 2 Peter, we also are told that Christians should view the end with joy rather than fear, and that there will be a new heaven and earth:

> Seeing then that all these things shall be dissolved, what manner of persons ought ye to be in all holy conversation and godliness, Looking for and hasting unto the coming of the day of God, wherein the heavens being on fire shall be dissolved, and the elements shall melt with fervent heat? Nevertheless we, according to his promise, look for new heavens and a new earth, wherein dwelleth righteousness. (2 Peter 3:11-13, KJV)

99. **Believers will have eternal life with God**

Bible passage: Matthew 25:31-46
Written: During the first century AD, about 2,000 years ago

In Matthew 25:31-46, we are told that during judgment day, non-believers and believers will be separated. The non-believers are symbolized by goats and the believers are symbolized by sheep.

The non-believers will face eternal punishment, but the believers will receive eternal life with God, as expressed in verse 46:

> And these shall go away into everlasting punishment: but the righteous into life eternal. (Matthew 25:46, KJV)

100. **All who believe in Jesus will be saved**

Bible passage: John 3:16-18
Written: During the first century AD, about 2,000 years ago

Many modern authors have written books about the end times, offering a variety of opinions, varying greatly in terms of their soundness, as to specific events that they believe will take place in the future. Some of the books have generated a great deal of hype and fear.

The Bible, however, is consistent and unwavering in what it says about the final outcome for each of us: People who believe in Jesus Christ are given the gift of salvation and eternal life with God. Here are some related verses from the Bible:

- For God so loved the world, that he gave his only begotten Son, that whosoever believeth in him should not perish, but have everlasting life. For God sent not his Son into the world to condemn the world; but that the world through him might be saved. He that believeth on him is not condemned: but he that believeth not is condemned already, because he hath not believed in the name of the only begotten Son of God. (John 3:16-18, KJV)

- For by grace are ye saved through faith; and that not of yourselves: it is the gift of God: Not of works, lest any man should boast. For we are his workmanship, created in Christ Jesus unto good works, which God hath before ordained that we should walk in them. (Ephesians 2:8-10, KJV)

- For all have sinned, and come short of the glory of God; Being justified freely by his grace through the redemption that is in Christ Jesus: (Romans 3:23,24, KJV)

- For the wages of sin is death; but the gift of God is eternal life through Jesus Christ our Lord. (Romans 6:23, KJV)

- Repent ye therefore, and be converted, that your sins may be blotted out, when the times of refreshing shall come from the presence of the Lord. (Acts 3:19, KJV)

- Be it known unto you all, and to all the people of Israel, that by the name of Jesus Christ . . . Neither is there salvation in any other: for there is none other name under heaven given among men, whereby we must be saved. (Acts 4:10,12, KJV)

- That if you confess with your mouth, "Jesus is Lord," and believe in your heart that God raised him from the dead, you will be saved. (Romans 10:9, NIV)

Closing thoughts

The research and commentaries featured within this book are the copyrighted work of George Konig and Ray Konig. It is our sincerest hope that the information is accurate and helpful.

If you have any suggestions as to how we might improve the material within our book, *100 Prophecies,* please contact us through our Web site at 100prophecies.com

We hope to hear from you. And we thank you for reading our book.

George Konig also is the author of *My Psalms,* a collection of Christian poetry available at www.konig.org.

More information about Christianity can be found at www.wels.net and at www.about-jesus.org.

- - -

For God so loved the world, that he gave his only begotten Son, that whosoever believeth in him should not perish, but have everlasting life. For God sent not his Son into the world to condemn the world; but that the world through him might be saved. He that believeth on him is not condemned: but he that believeth not is condemned already, because he hath not believed in the name of the only begotten Son of God. (John 3:16-18, KJV)

That if you confess with your mouth, "Jesus is Lord," and believe in your heart that God raised him from the dead, you will be saved. (Romans 10:9, NIV)

Christian beliefs

Many Christian churches recognize three ancient creeds as accurate expressions of Bible teaching: the Apostles' Creed, the Nicene Creed, and the Athanasian Creed. These creeds often are recited during worship services by Christians.

The three creeds can be found on the following pages. The Wisconsin Evangelical Lutheran Synod offers this information about the creeds:

> The Apostles' Creed is a brief statement of gospel truths taught by the apostles. It was not formulated by theologians, but out of the needs of the Christian church. Christians used it to tell others what they believed and also to confess their faith with one another as they met for worship.
> Source: http://www.wels.net/what-we-believe/statements-beliefs/apostles-creed
>
> The Nicene Creed was written around A.D. 325 in defense of the true Christian faith. The Council at Nicea developed it, expanding on the deity of Christ, in order to safeguard the apostles' teaching.
> Source: http://www.wels.net/what-we-believe/statements-beliefs/nicene-creed
>
> This creed [The Athanasian Creed] is named after St. Athanasius, a staunch defender of the Christian faith in the fourth century. It was prepared to assist the Church in combating two errors that undermined Bible teaching. One error denied that God's Son and the Holy Spirit are of one being or Godhead with the Father. The other error denied that Jesus Christ is true God and true man in one person. The Athanasian Creed continues to serve the Christian Church as a standard of the truth. It declares that whoever rejects

> the doctrine of the Trinity and the doctrine of Christ is without the saving faith.
> Source: http://www.wels.net/what-we-believe/statements-beliefs/athanasian-creed

More information about the creeds, and more information about Christianity, is available at wels.net.

Apostles' Creed

I believe in God, the Father almighty,
maker of heaven and earth.

I believe in Jesus Christ, his only Son, our Lord,
who was conceived by the Holy Spirit
born of the virgin Mary,
suffered under Pontius Pilate,
was crucified, died, and was buried.
He descended into hell.
The third day he rose again from the dead.
He ascended into heaven
and is seated at the right hand of God the Father almighty.
From there he will come to judge the living and the dead.

I believe in the Holy Spirit,
the holy Christian Church,
the communion of saints,
the forgiveness of sins,
the resurrection of the body,
and the life everlasting. Amen.

Note: The reference to Jesus as having "descended into hell" might be based on the Bible passage found in 1 Peter 3:18-20. In the introductory pages of *The Concordia Self-Study Bible NIV,* an explanation of the Apostles' Creed says that Jesus descended into hell "not to suffer or to offer deceased souls a second chance, but to proclaim his lordship." The Apostles' Creed is not contained in the Bible. It is the work of early Christians who intended to create a summary, based on various Bible passages, to explain to others what it means to be a Christian.

Nicene Creed

We believe in one God, the Father, the Almighty,
maker of heaven and earth,
of all that is,
seen and unseen.

We believe in one Lord, Jesus Christ, the only Son of God,
eternally begotten of the Father,
God from God, Light from Light, true God from true God,
begotten, not made,
of one being with the Father.
Through him all things were made.
For us and for our salvation, he came down from heaven,
was incarnate of the Holy Spirit and the virgin Mary,
and became fully human.
For our sake he was crucified under Pontius Pilate.
He suffered death and was buried.
On the third day he rose again in accordance with the Scriptures.
He ascended into heaven
and is seated at the right hand of the Father.
He will come again in glory to judge the living and the dead,
and his kingdom will have no end.

We believe in the Holy Spirit,
the Lord, the giver of life,
who proceeds from the Father and the Son,
who in unity with the Father and the Son is worshiped and glorified,
who has spoken through the prophets.
We believe in one holy Christian and apostolic Church.
We acknowledge one baptism for the forgiveness of sins.
We look for the resurrection of the dead
and the life of the world to come. Amen.

Athanasian Creed

Whoever wishes to be saved must, above all else, hold to the true Christian faith. Whoever does not keep this faith pure in all points will certainly perish forever.

Now this is the true Christian faith: We worship one God in three persons and three persons in one God, without mixing the persons or dividing the divine being. For each person—the Father, the Son, and the Holy Spirit—is distinct, but the deity of Father, Son, and Holy Spirit is one, equal in glory and coeternal in majesty. What the Father is, so is the Son, and so is the Holy Spirit. The Father is uncreated, the Son uncreated, the Holy Spirit uncreated; the Father is infinite, the Son infinite, the Holy Spirit infinite; the Father is eternal, the Son eternal, the Holy Spirit eternal; yet they are not three who are eternal, but there is one who is eternal, just as they are not three who are uncreated, nor three who are infinite, but there is one who is uncreated and one who is infinite. In the same way the Father is almighty, the Son is almighty, and the Holy Spirit is almighty; yet they are not three who are almighty, but there is one who is almighty. So the Father is God, the Son is God, the Holy Spirit is God; yet they are not three Gods, but one God. So the Father is Lord, the Son is Lord, the Holy Spirit is Lord; yet they are not three Lords, but one Lord. For just as Christian truth compels us to confess each person individually to be God and Lord, so the true Christian faith forbids us to speak of three Gods or three Lords. The Father is neither made nor created nor begotten of anyone. The Son is neither made nor created, but is begotten of the Father alone. The Holy Spirit is neither made nor created nor begotten, but proceeds from the Father and the Son. So there is one Father, not three Fathers; one Son, not three Sons; one Holy Spirit, not three Holy Spirits. And within this Trinity none comes before or after; none is greater or inferior, but all three persons are coequal and coeternal, so that in every way, as stated before, all three persons are to be worshiped as one God and one God worshiped as three persons. Whoever wishes to be saved must have this conviction of the Trinity.

It is furthermore necessary for eternal salvation truly to believe that our Lord Jesus Christ also took on human flesh. Now this is the true Christian faith: We believe and confess that our Lord Jesus Christ, God's Son, is both God and man. He is God, eternally begotten from the nature of the Father, and he is man, born in time from the nature of his mother, fully God, fully man, with rational soul and human flesh, equal to the Father as to his deity, less than the Father as to his humanity; and though he is both God and Man, Christ is not two persons but one, one, not by changing the deity into flesh, but by taking the humanity into God; one, indeed, not by mixture of the natures, but by unity in one person;

for just as the rational soul and flesh are one human being, so God and man are one Christ. He suffered for our salvation, descended into hell, rose the third day from the dead. He ascended into heaven, is seated at the right hand of God the Father almighty, and from there he will come to judge the living and the dead. At his coming all people will rise with their own bodies to answer for their personal deeds. Those who have done good will enter eternal life, but those who have done evil will go into eternal fire.

This is the true Christian faith. Whoever does not faithfully and firmly believe this cannot be saved.

Bibliography

Chapter 1

Item 2: J. Barton Payne, *Encyclopedia of Biblical Prophecy.* Grand Rapids, Michigan: Baker Book House. 1987. Page 13 and the Statistical Appendix.

Item 6: China Daily. 2008. *DNA test to clarify Confucius confusion.* On-line. Available from Internet, http://english.peopledaily.com.cn/200606/20/eng20060620_275518.html, accessed September 7, 2008.

Item 6: Mayell, Hillary. February 14, 2003. *Genghis Khan.* National Geographic News. On-line. Available from Internet, http://news.nationalgeographic.com/news/pf/36013605.html, accessed August 24, 2008.

Item 7: Edersheim, Alfred. *The Life and Times of Jesus the Messiah.* Book II. Chapter V. Volume I. London: Longmans, Green, and Co. 1883. Page 163.

Chapter 2

Item 14: Josephus, *Antiquities of the Jews,* Book IX, Chapter 11. As taken from: *The Works of Flavius Josephus.* Translator: William Whiston. Halifax: Milner and Sowerby. 1864. Page 214.

Item 17: Josephus. *The Wars of the Jews,* Book VII, Chapter 8.

Item 17: *The Babylonian Talmud.* Tract Taanith, Chapter 4.

Chapter 3

Item 24: Justin Martyr. *The First Apology of Justin,* Chapter XXXII. As taken from: *The Ante-Nicene Fathers.* Translations of The Writings of the Fathers Down to A.D. 325. Editors: The Rev. Alexander Roberts, D.D., and James Donaldson, LL.D. American Reprint of the Edinburgh Edition. Revised and chronologically arranged, with brief prefaces and occasional notes, by A. Cleveland Coxe, D.D. Volume I. The Apostolic Fathers.— Justin Martyr. — Irenaeus. Buffalo, New York: The Christian Literature Publishing Company. 1885. Page 174.

Item 26: R. Laird Harris, et al, *Theological Wordbook of the Old Testament.* Volume 2. Page 672. Chicago: Moody Press. 1980.

Item 28: Justin Martyr. *The First Apology of Justin,* Chapter XXXII. As taken from: *The Ante-Nicene Fathers.* Translations of The Writings of the Fathers Down to A.D. 325. Editors: The Rev. Alexander Roberts, D.D., and James Donaldson, LL.D. American Reprint of the Edinburgh Edition. Revised and chronologically arranged, with brief prefaces and occasional notes, by A. Cleveland Coxe, D.D. Volume I. The Apostolic Fathers.— Justin Martyr. — Irenaeus. Buffalo, New York: The Christian Literature Publishing Company. 1885. Page 173.

Item 28: Babylonian Talmud, Tract Sanhedrin, Chapter XI, as translated by H. Freedman, under the editorship of Rabbi Dr. I. Epstein.

Chapter 4

Item 31: Josephus, *Antiquities of the Jews,* Book XVIII, Chapter 5. As taken from: *The Works of Flavius Josephus.*

Translator: William Whiston. Halifax: Milner and Sowerby. 1864. Page 396.

Item 32: Irenaeus. *Against Heresies,* Book II, Chapter 22. As taken from: *The Ante-Nicene Fathers.* Translations of The Writings of the Fathers Down to A.D. 325. Editors: The Rev. Alexander Roberts, D.D., and James Donaldson, LL.D. American Reprint of the Edinburgh Edition. Revised and chronologically arranged, with brief prefaces and occasional notes, by A. Cleveland Coxe, D.D. Volume I. The Apostolic Fathers.— Justin Martyr. — Irenaeus. Buffalo, New York: The Christian Literature Publishing Company. 1885. Page 390.

Item 35: Edersheim, Alfred. *The Life and Times of Jesus the Messiah.* Appendix IX. Volume II. London: Longmans, Green, and Co. 1883. Page 732.

Item 35: *Babylonian Talmud,* Tract Sanhedrin, Chapter XI, as translated by Rabbi Michael L. Rodkinson in 1903. First printed in 1918.

Item 39: *Babylonian Talmud,* Tract Sanhedrin, Chapter XI, as translated by H. Freedman, under the editorship of Rabbi Dr. I. Epstein.

Item 39: *The Fifty-Third Chapter of Isaiah According to the Jewish Interpreters,* Volume II, Chapter XXXVII, with translations by S.R. Driver and A. Neubauer. From an electronic edition, Copyright © 2005 by Varda Books, that is based on the printed edition originally published in 1876.

Chapter 5

Item 46: Charles Augustus Briggs, D.D. *Messianic Prophecy: The Prediction of the Fulfilment of Redemption*

Through the Messiah. New York: Charles Scribner's Sons. 1889. Pages 326, 327.

Chapter 6

Item 52: *Babylonian Talmud,* Tract Yomah, Chapter IV, as translated by Rabbi Michael L. Rodkinson.

Chapter 7

Item 61: Josephus, *The Wars of the Jews,* Book VII, Chapter 8. As taken from: *The Works of Flavius Josephus.* Translator: William Whiston. Halifax: Milner and Sowerby. 1864. Pages 627-628.

Item 62: Josephus, *The Wars of the Jews,* Book VI, Chapter 9. As taken from: *The Works of Flavius Josephus.* Translator: William Whiston. Halifax: Milner and Sowerby. 1864. Page 612.

Item 62: Eusebius. *The Church History of Eusebius,* Book IV, Chapter 6. As translated in *A Select Library of Nicene and Post-Nicene Fathers of the Christian Church, Second Series,* Volume 1. Edited by Philip Schaff, D.D., LL.D., and Henry Wace, D.D. New York: Christian Literature Publishing Co., 1890. Page 177.

Item 63: Dio, Cassius. *Roman History,* Book 69. As taken from: *Dio's Rome.* Fifth Volume (Extant books 61-76). Translated by Herbert Baldwin Foster. Troy, New York: Pafraets Book Company. 1906. Page 227.

Item 64: Pliny. *Pliny's Epistle to Trajan, About A.D. 112,* as translated by William Whiston. As taken from: *The Works of Flavius Josephus.* Translator: William Whiston. Halifax: Milner and Sowerby. 1864. Page 685.

Item 65: *The First Epistle of Clement to the Corinthians,* Chapter V. As taken from: *The Ante-Nicene Fathers.* Translations of The Writings of the Fathers Down to A.D. 325. Editors: The Rev. Alexander Roberts, D.D., and James Donaldson, LL.D. American Reprint of the Edinburgh Edition. Revised and chronologically arranged, with brief prefaces and occasional notes, by A. Cleveland Coxe, D.D. Volume I. The Apostolic Fathers.— Justin Martyr. — Irenaeus. Buffalo, New York: The Christian Literature Publishing Company. 1885. Page 6.

Item 70: Russell Ash, *Top 10 of Everything 2007.* London: Octopus Publishing Group Ltd. 2006. Page 96.

Item 70: United Bible Societies. January 23, 2007. *2006 Scripture Language Report.* On-line. Available from Internet, http://www.biblesociety.org/latestnews/latest390.html, and specifically at http://www.biblesociety.org/latestnews/latest390.pdf, accessed September 15, 2008.

Chapter 8

Item 73: *The Historical Library of Diodorus the Sicilian,* Book II, Chapter 2. Translated by G. Booth. London: W. McDowall. 1814. Page 122.

Item 74: *The Historical Library of Diodorus the Sicilian,* Book II, Chapter 2. Translated by G. Booth. London: W. McDowall. 1814. Page 123.

Item 75: Nineveh. (2008). In Encyclopædia Britannica. Retrieved September 26, 2008, from Encyclopædia Britannica Online:

http://www.britannica.com/EBchecked/topic/415684/Nineveh

Item 76: Austen Henry Layard. *Nineveh and Its Remains.* London: John Murray, Albemarle Street. 1867. Page xix within the Introduction section.

Item 78: Herodotus, *The Histories* Volume I, Book I, Section 191. Translated by G.C. Macaulay and revised by Donald Lateiner. Spark Educational Publishing. 2004. Page 69.

Item 80: Ian Shaw and Robert Jameson. *A Dictionary of Archaeology.* Blackwell Publishing. 2002. Page 100.

Chapter 9

Item 81: *Concordia Self-Study Bible New International Version.* General editor: Robert G. Hoerber. Footnote for Daniel 2:32-43. St. Louis: Concordia Publishing House. Page 1305.

Item 81: *Concordia Self-Study Bible New International Version.* General editor: Robert G. Hoerber. Footnote for Daniel 2:44. St. Louis: Concordia Publishing House. Page 1305.

Item 85: Rawlinson, George. *History of Phoenicia.* Chapter XIV. London: Longmans, Green, and Co. 1889. Pages 514 and 520-521.

Item 86: Benjamin Of Tudela. *The Itinerary Of Benjamin Of Tudela.* New York: Philipp Feldheim, Inc. 1907. Page 31.

Item 86: Tyre. (2008). In Columbia Encyclopedia, Sixth

Edition. Retrieved September 26, 2008, from Columbia Encyclopedia online: http://www.encyclopedia.com/doc/1E1-Tyre.html

Item 88: Josephus, *Antiquities of the Jews,* Book XII, Chapter 8. As taken from: *The Works of Flavius Josephus.* Translator: William Whiston. Halifax: Milner and Sowerby. 1864. Page 268.

Item 88: Josephus, *Antiquities of the Jews,* Book XIII, Chapter 9. As taken from: *The Works of Flavius Josephus.* Translator: William Whiston. Halifax: Milner and Sowerby. 1864. Page 288.

Item 88: JewishEncyclopedia.com. *EDOM, IDUMEA.* On-line. Available from Internet, http://jewishencyclopedia.com/view.jsp?artid=45&letter=E, accessed August 26, 2008.

Item 89: Robinson, George L. *The Biblical World.* Editor: William R. Harper. Chicago: The University of Chicago Press. 1901. Page 6.

Item 89: Alexander Crawford Lindsay Crawford. *Letters on Egypt, Edom, and the Holy Land.* London: Bell & Daldy. 1866. Letter III. Pages 232 and 233.